The Age Factor in Second Language Acquisition

Multilingual Matters

Approaches to Second Language Acquisition
R. TOWELL and R. HAWKINS
Culture and Language Learning in Higher Education
MICHAEL BYRAM (ed.)
Distance Education for Language Teachers
RON HOWARD and IAN McGRATH (eds)
French for Communication 1979-1990
ROY DUNNING
Languages in Contact and Conflict
SUE WRIGHT (ed.)
Language Reclamation
HUBISI NWENMELY
A Parents' and Teachers' Guide to Bilingualism
COLIN BAKER
Policy and Practices in Bilingual Education
O. GARCÍA and C. BAKER (eds)
Quantifying Language
PHIL SCHOLFIELD
Reflections on Language Learning
L. BARBARA and M. SCOTT (eds)
Tasks and Language Learning
GRAHAM CROOKES and SUSAN M. GASS (eds)
Tasks in a Pedagogical Context
GRAHAM CROOKES and SUSAN M. GASS (eds)
Teaching-and-Learning Language-and-Culture
MICHAEL BYRAM, CAROL MORGAN and colleagues
Teaching Science to Language Minority Students
JUDITH W. ROSENTHAL
Validation in Language Testing
A. CUMMING and R. BERWICK (eds)

Please contact us for the latest book information:
Multilingual Matters Ltd,
Frankfurt Lodge, Clevedon Hall, Victoria Road,
Clevedon, Avon, England, BS21 7SJ

The Age Factor in Second Language Acquisition

A Critical Look at the Critical Period Hypothesis

Edited by

David Singleton and Zsolt Lengyel

MULTILINGUAL MATTERS LTD
Clevedon • Philadelphia • Adelaide

IN MEMORIAM

To the memory of our much-missed fathers

Imre Lengyel *1910–1978*
Stanley Leonard Singleton *1907–1992*

Library of Congress Cataloging in Publication Data

The Age Factor in Second Language Acquisition/
Edited by David Singleton and Zsolt Lengyel.
1. Second language acquisition–Age factors–Congresses.
I. Singleton, D.M. (David Michael). II. Lengyel, Zsolt.
P118.2.A35 1995
418–dc20 95-20841

British Library Cataloguing in Publication Data

A CIP catalogue record for this book is available from the British Library.

ISBN 1-85359-302-8 (hbk)
ISBN 1-85359-301-X (pbk)

Multilingual Matters Ltd

UK: Frankfurt Lodge, Clevedon Hall, Victoria Road, Clevedon, Avon BS21 7SJ.
USA: 1900 Frost Road, Suite 101, Bristol, PA 19007, USA.
Australia: P.O. Box 6025, 83 Gilles Street, Adelaide, SA 5000, Australia.

Printed and bound in Great Britain by the Cromwell Press.

Contents

Foreword

This book has its origins in two conferences, one of which did not happen, and one of which did! In 1991 one of the editors of the present volume, Zsolt Lengyel, offered to host an 'expert seminar' on the age factor in second language acquisition for the European Second Language Association (EUROSLA), and the other of the present editors, David Singleton (then Secretary of EUROSLA) was asked to assist in the organisation of this event. The view of EUROSLA was that, given the theoretical discussion that was in train concerning differences in language capacity, including differential access to putative innate endowments, in children and adults, and given, at a more practical level, the widespread revival of enthusiasm for foreign language programmes at primary school level, the time was ripe for an exchange of expert views on the age question. EUROSLA was also keen to involve itself in East–West co-operation within Europe and to participate in the opening of channels of communication relative to language learning and teaching between previously separated parts of the continent. Unfortunately, as things turned out, it proved impossible, for various reasons, to bring together the invited contributors to the seminar at the time and in the venue envisaged. However, the idea of gathering a variety of informed perspectives on the topic of age in second language development was retained.

This idea was reinforced by the experience of a conference which *did* take place, namely, the Fourteenth Annual Meeting of the American Association for Applied Linguistics (Seattle, February–March, 1992), which included a symposium on the critical period involving some of the EUROSLA-connected individuals originally targeted for the expert seminar, and at which, coincidentally, some other papers on this issue were presented. The interest in such papers and in the symposium itself was very considerable, and so the notion that a multifaceted treatment of the age question would meet a certain need — or at least a certain curiosity — appeared to be confirmed.

In the fullness of time those who had originally agreed in principle to take part in the EUROSLA seminar plus some of those who had presented age-related papers in Seattle were invited to consider contributing chapters to a compilation of articles on the Critical Period Hypothesis in the context of second language acquisition. When the submissions resulting from this invitation were scrutinised, it was discovered that in all cases they contained elements of scepticism or qualification *vis-à-vis* strong or absolutist versions of the Critical Period Hypothesis. This was extremely convenient, since the problem of finding an overarching theme for the proposed book was thereby immediately solved. The subtitle of the volume, *A Critical Look at the Critical Period Hypothesis*, thus more or less wrote itself.

It needs perhaps to be made clear that although, as has been explained, two conferences were very much bound up with the genesis of this collection, the book is not a set of proceedings. Certain aspects of the articles it contains bear, in some cases, a relationship to elements of previous oral presentations, but in every instance these articles have been prepared specifically with this particular volume in mind. Accordingly, a very large proportion of the material presented and the discussion conducted between these covers will have been neither heard nor seen anywhere else.

Our thanks are due to Vivian Cook for coming up with the idea of specialist debates on topics in second language acquisition research within the EUROSLA framework — and indeed for coming up with the idea of EUROSLA in the first place! We are also indebted to Barbara Freed for some extremely helpful advice she provided during the initial stages of putting the book together. We also wish to acknowledge the support and encouragement we have received in this venture from our friends and colleagues in EUROSLA and in our respective universities, and to express our gratitude to Marjukka and Mike Grover of Multilingual Matters Ltd for their swift and sustaining responses to our proposals in respect of this volume. Finally, we must thank Emer and Christopher Singleton for their invaluable practical assistance in the preparation of the typescript.

We are acutely aware of the fact that — partly because of the way in which it came into being — the product for which we are responsible does not offer anything resembling an integrated approach to the issue of the age factor in second language acquisition. This is from one point of view a weakness, but, on the other hand, to the extent that the disparateness of the perspectives the book contains in fact reflects the true state of play in this area of second language research, one can at least credit the volume with representativeness. We trust, in any case, that the arguments and findings set out in the book, diverse though they be, will, severally and cumulatively, have some influence in promoting an optique on the Critical Period

Hypothesis which resists the temptations of sweeping statement and reductionism.

By way of a suitably mischievous *envoi*, the following quotation from Wordsworth's *The Fountain* seems apposite:

The wiser mind
Mourns less for what age takes away
Than what it leaves behind.

David Singleton, *Dublin, December 1994*
Zsolt Lengyel, *Veszprém, December 1994*

Introduction: A Critical Look at the Critical Period Hypothesis in Second Language Acquisition Research

DAVID SINGLETON

The Age Factor Debate: Contention and Consensus

The issue of whether the age at which individuals begin to be exposed to languages other than their native languages plays a role in the manner in which, and/or the success with which, they come to grips with the new languages in question, has been a perennial theme of discussion amongst researchers, educators and indeed learners for a very long time indeed. Nor has interest in the topic waned, to judge from the number of publications that continue to appear on the topic. The reasons for this widespread and undiminished interest in the age question are manifold, relating not just to theoretical issues such as whether a putative innate language faculty continues to function beyond a particular maturational point (see, e.g., the contributions in this volume from Cook, from Ioup, and from Martohardjono & Flynn), but also to very practical issues such as when second language instruction should begin — an important question at present in the light of the recent renewal of enthusiasm in various countries for the introduction of second languages into the primary school curriculum (see, e.g., CMIEB/CLA/Ville de Besançon, 1992; J. Harris, 1992; Johnstone, 1991; Pincemin & O'Neil, 1990; Titone, 1986; Vilke & Vrhovac, 1993)

A great variety of views have been expressed on the age question, ranging from the position that children are in all respects more efficient and effective second language learners than adults to the exactly contrary position that adolescents and adults are in all respects more efficient and effective second language learners than children (see Singleton, 1989: Chapter 4). It is also worth noting that there has been a certain amount of intra-researcher variation with regard to opinions offered on this issue, with somewhat different views being proposed by the same individuals at different points in time. For example, the present author — to name but one! — adopted a very much more sceptical attitude to the notion of an age factor in second language acquisition in his earlier treatment of the subject (Singleton, 1981) than he has done in subsequent publications (e.g. Singleton, 1989, 1992a).

In these last-mentioned publications Singleton's stance is that the balance of evidence relative to age and second language learning broadly favours the eventual attainment-focused line taken by Krashen, Long & Scarcella (1979), namely, that in situations of 'naturalistic' exposure, while older beginners tend to outperform their juniors — at least in some respects — in the initial stages of learning, in terms of long-term outcomes, generally speaking, the earlier exposure to the target language begins the better. This position has been widely and increasingly acknowledged, even by those who might earlier have had a different view, as the one which best fits the totality of evidence, and it can probably now be characterised as the 'consensus view' (see, e.g., Cook, 1991; Ellis, 1994; Harley, 1986; Long, 1990). Powerful empirical support for the Krashen *et al.* position comes from studies carried out by Snow and Hoefnagel-Höhle (e.g. 1978a, 1978b) which investigated the development in Dutch of 69 English-speaking residents in the Netherlands; these studies provide clear evidence of more rapid learning on the part of adult and adolescent subjects in the early stages and of younger beginners catching up on and beginning to outstrip their elders after a year or so.

As far as instructed second language learning is concerned, the consistent finding which has emerged from studies of the results of primary/elementary school second language programmes (see, e.g., Burstall, Jamieson, Cohen & Hargreaves, 1974; Oller & Nagato, 1974) is that pupils who are given early exposure to a second language and are then integrated into classes containing pupils without such experience do not maintain a clear advantage for more than a relatively short period over pupils who begin to learn the language only at secondary level. The apparent discrepancy between such evidence from school-based studies and evidence from naturalistic studies can, however, probably be related to the blurring effect resulting from mixing beginners and non-beginners in the same classes (see, e.g., Stern, 1976; Singleton, 1992a) and can, in any case, readily be accounted for in terms of gross differences in exposure time between naturalistic and instructed learners.

As far as the latter explanation is concerned, clearly, a period of, say, five years of exposure to a second language in a second language environment would in most circumstances involve a very great deal more exposure to the language than five years of formal second-language instruction, where the target language was being treated simply as one school subject among many. Thus, if the amount-of-exposure variable is held constant, the concepts of 'initial advantage' and 'eventual attainment' in a formal instructional setting need to be associated with much longer real-time periods than in a largely informal exposure situation. To be more precise, the present author has estimated (Singleton, 1989: 236) that more than 18 years would need to be spent in a formal instructional setting in order to obtain the same amount of second language input as seems (according to the Snow and Hoefnagel-Höhle studies) to be required for older learners' 'initial advantage' to begin to disappear. No one would want to postulate a literal equation between a given quantity of input over 12 months and the same amount of exposure over 18 years, but the point is that when comparing different categories of language learners one does have always to keep in mind the varying relationship between real time and exposure time.

Short-term studies of instructed second language learning (e.g. Ekstrand, 1978) have indicated the same kind of initial advantage for older beginners as short-term studies of naturalistic L2 learning. Singleton (1989, 1992a) has suggested, in the light of the above-discussed differences in density of L2 experience, that this initial advantage of older learners, which in the naturalistic learning situation appears to last about a year, may, under the régime of vastly sparser exposure of the formal learning situation, last for several years. This would readily account for the effect within the normal secondary-school cycle of pupils without primary-level L2 instruction 'catching up' with pupils who have received such instruction. On this view, the eventual benefits of early second language learning in a formal instructional environment might be expected to show up only in rather longer-term studies than have to date been attempted.

Second Language Evidence and the Critical Period Hypothesis

The upshot of discussion in the previous section is that both naturalistic evidence and formal instructional evidence can be interpreted as being consistent with what may be termed the 'younger = better in the long run' view. This looks like good news for proponents of the Critical Period Hypothesis (CPH), recently summarised by Breathnach (1993: 43) as follows:

> During development there are periods of special sensibility related to particular elements in the environment towards which the organism is directed with an irresistible impulse and a well-defined activity. These periods, which help the organism to acquire certain functions or characteristics are ephemeral. In language, above all else, the transitory sensitive period is vital...

The notion that second language evidence supports the CPH needs, however, to be qualified in at least two ways.

First, it is perfectly obvious from what has already been said that the available empirical evidence cannot be taken to license the simplistic 'younger = better in all circumstances over any timescale' version of the CPH that one finds in folk wisdom and that seems to underlie some of the 'classic' treatments of age and second-language learning (e.g. Tomb, 1925; Stengel, 1939; Penfield & Roberts, 1959; Lenneberg, 1967). Everything points to the situation being very much more complex and very much more interesting than such treatments would tend to suggest.

Second, even the 'younger = better in the long run' version of the CPH in respect of second-language learning needs to be seen in the perspective of a general tendency and not as an absolute, immutable law. Both research and the informal observations of those who are in daily contact with second-language learners suggest that an early start in a second language is neither a strictly necessary nor a universally sufficient condition for the attainment of native-like proficiency. Given the enormous variation in people's experience of second languages — even (or especially!) in the classroom (see, e.g., Dabène, 1990) — this ought to be a truism. One notes that even Penfield, an early high priest of the CPH (see Dechert's contribution to the present volume) was prepared to recognise that under some circumstances an individual adult beginner *may* become a 'master' of his/her target second language (Penfield & Roberts, 1959: 24), and the recent literature on early bilingualism strongly indicates that the age at which one first encounters a second language is only one of the determinants of the ultimate level of proficiency attained in that language (see, e.g., Romaine, 1989: 232–244).

The papers collected in the present volume essentially provide expansions of and additional arguments for the above qualifications. In their various ways and proceeding from very diverse points of departure, they converge on a version of the CPH which steers clear of rigid determinism, which calls into doubt the possibility of neatly separating the second language from the first in psycholinguistic terms, which admits of the possibility of differential effects arising from variation amongst learners and amongst learning situations, and which refuses to envisage the second language learning enterprise as a monolith.

Age and Different Aspects of Second Language Acquisition: Morphosyntax and Phonology

The reference above to the non-monolithic nature of second language acquisition prompts a consideration of how the 'consensus view' of the role of age in this context stands in relation to the different 'levels' of language.

Krashen *et al.* were careful in their 1979 statement of their position to restrict what they had to say about the initial advantage of older learners to the realm of morphosyntax:

(1) Adults proceed through early stages of syntactic and morphological development faster than children (where time and exposure are held constant).
(2) Older children acquire faster than younger children (again, early stages of syntactic and morphological development where time and exposure are held constant). (Krashen *et al.*, 1979, reprint: 161)

This contrasts with the unrestricted application, in terms of different areas of language, of what they have to say about eventual attainment:

(3) Acquirers who begin natural exposure to second languages during childhood generally achieve higher second language proficiency than those beginning as adults.

The reason for Krashen *et al.*'s caution was simply that, whereas the long-term advantages of an early start seemed to be evidenced across the board in naturalistic studies, findings in relation to short-term outcomes appeared mixed. As far as morphosyntax was concerned, the evidence on an initial advantage for older learners was overwhelming, but data in respect of phonological acquisition were difficult to interpret, and data in respect of lexical acquisition were scarce and were also characterised by some inconsistency. Actually, the state of the evidence is still substantially as Krashen *et al.* found it to be. The remainder of the present section discusses morphosyntactic and phonological development in this connection in a little more detail; the much-neglected lexical question is dealt with separately in the next section.

The one study which appears to yield counter-evidence to the claim that the second language morphosyntactic development of older learners is faster than that of younger learners is Kessler & Idar's (1979) investigation of the morphological development in English of a Vietnamese woman refugee and her 4-year-old daughter during the first months of their residence in Texas. In this case the child is claimed by Kessler & Idar to have shown vastly more rapid progress than her mother. However, this finding needs to be qualified in two ways. First, Kessler & Idar's study had serious design flaws: the two testing periods for the child were four months further apart than those for the mother, which means that there was a marked difference in the exposure times involved — in the daughter's favour. Second, there were particular affective–attitudinal factors involved: the two subjects were refugees rather than ordinary immigrants. Kessler & Idar (1979: 78) themselves stress 'the role of affective variables and the retarding effect of negative attitudes arising from difficult adjustments to a new culture', and it is at least permissible to speculate that an adult refugee will experience difficulties of adjustment more acutely than a child will.

All other available evidence shows older learners initially moving ahead more swiftly in their acquisition of second language morphosyntax. The evidence also indicates, however, that younger learners tend in the long run to outperform their elders in this sphere as in other spheres. Snow and Hoefnagel-Höhle's (1978a, b) studies can again be cited in this connection, as well as longer-term studies such as that of Patkowski (1980). Patkowski's study examined the English syntactic proficiency — as assessed by two trained judges — of 67 highly educated immigrants, all of whom had resided in the United States for at least five years. It found a strong negative relationship between age of arrival and syntactic rating. In addition, the ratings for the 33 subjects who had entered the United States before age 15 were found to bunch rather dramatically at the upper end of the scale, whereas those for the 34 subjects who had arrived after that age there was a strikingly 'normal' curve.

Something which is absent from many empirical treatments of age and second language development is the question of whether there might be qualitatively different areas within the morphosyntactic dimension of second language acquisition. If it is the case that innate principles and parameters — such as those envisaged by Chomskyan Universal Grammar (UG) — guide certain aspects of language acquisition, then those areas of grammar on which such innate principles and parameters bear presumably need to be distinguished from language-particular morphosyntactic elements which develop — alongside and in interaction with language-particular aspects of the lexicon — unaided by any inborn guidance system. The question which then arises is whether the innate principles in question remain available throughout life and are operative during second language acquisition . If they do remain available, it follows that the parts of second language grammatical development which they inform ought not to be affected by the age factor, whatever may be the situation in relation to other aspects (for discussion of this point in the present volume, see especially Martohardjono & Flynn's contribution).

This is not to suggest that any distinction along the above lines will be easy to make, nor that the question of whether innate principles remain available will be easy to settle. With reference to the latter point, the complexities and difficulties of the argument are well illustrated by Bley-Vroman's recent defence of a modified version of his Fundamental Difference Hypothesis (FDH), in which he claims that UG is *not* operative in late second language acquisition but that late second language learners are nevertheless able to derive UG-like principles from other, general cognitive, sources and thus to 'treat L2 as grammar':

> If one posits that learners 'treat L2 as grammar'...then the philosophical and empirical objections to the FDH largely disappear. Specifically,... 'UG effects' may be expected, even in the absence of a UG-created grammar. (Bley-Vroman, 1994, abstract: 7)

Before such subtlety even a thirteenth-century scholastic theologian might be prepared to take off his hat!

Further points for serious consideration in this context emerge from a critique of the work of Johnson and Newport (Johnson & Newport, 1989; Johnson, 1992) by Kellerman (forthcoming). Kellerman casts doubt on the assumption that a non-native speaker assessing a sentence in a grammaticality judgment test will necessarily focus on the same feature or features as a native speaker would react to. He also points out that in grammaticality judgment tests there may be instances where the variables of formal correctness/deviancy and functional plausibility/implausibility are fatally confounded. He goes on to suggest, citing Van Wuijtswinkel (1994), that there is an interaction between age and language background in the learning of second language grammar, with first language analogues allowing certain second language features to be acquired at any age.

In any case, we should be clear that any age-related advantage in relation to second language morphosyntactic development is no more than a general tendency. Time and again it emerges from research that some learners who begin late seem to do as well as early beginners. Thus, in the above-mentioned study by Patkowski, five of the 34 subjects who had entered the United States after age 15 scored in precisely the same range as the majority of those who had arrived before age 15. The case studies reported by Ioup in the present volume should also give pause to anyone tempted towards absolutism in this connection.

Turning now to the question of second language phonological development, a few contextualising remarks will suffice here, since the relevant research is repeatedly referred to in the chapters which follow — and is reviewed fairly comprehensively in Chapter 1, by Bongaerts, Planken & Schils.

One point which immediately becomes obvious from the most cursory glance at the literature is that the evidence in relation to short-term age-effects in this area presents some difficulties of interpretation. Thus, while some studies of a short/short-to-medium term character appear to show an advantage for younger beginners (e.g. Dunkel & Pillet, 1957; Fathman, 1975; Tahta, Wood & Loewenthal, 1981), others appear to show quite the opposite (e.g. Ekstrand, 1978; Ervin-Tripp, 1974; Olson & Samuels, 1973).

With regard to longer-term effects, an especially interesting piece of research is a study of English-speakers' naturalistic acquisition of Dutch by Snow & Hoefnagel-Höhle (1977) — in the same series as those already mentioned but focusing specifically on phonology. This particular investigation had both a cross-sectional and a longitudinal component. In the cross-sectional component 136 subjects aged from 5 to 31 years were tested on multiple imitations of Dutch words early in their stay in the Netherlands, and in the longitudinal component 47 subjects ranging in age from 3 to 60 had their Dutch pronunciation assessed in both imitation and spontaneous production conditions at four- to five-month intervals. The results of the cross-sectional component showed a linear improvement of scores with age. The longitudinal component, on the other hand, showed an initial advantage for older subjects but a rapid catching up by the younger learners — to the extent that they were outperforming the adults on some of the sounds after a period of 10 to 11 months' learning and after 18 months had apparently overtaken the adults in terms of overall scores. These findings, which are broadly in line with those of Snow & Hoefnagel-Höhle's (1978a, b) studies, clearly suggest that, if older learners have an initial advantage in relation to second language phonology, any such advantage is short-lived.

Other long-term naturalistic studies confirm this. A whole range of research based on long-stay immigrant subjects — including the much-cited investigations of Asher & García (1969) and Seliger, Krashen & Ladefoged (1975) — indicate that the earlier an immigrant arrives in the host country and begins to be exposed to its language the more likely he/she is to end up sounding like a native. It should perhaps be re-emphasised, however, that here, as in the case of morphosyntactic development, what is in question is a tendency rather than an absolute rule. In both of the above-cited studies, for example, a small minority of the late arrivals (about 7% in each case) diverged from the overall pattern and behaved as if they were early arrivals.

As with morphosyntax, so with phonology too, a question that has been too rarely asked is whether it is justified to talk about the acquisition of a more or less self-contained, more or less unitary area of L2 proficiency. This issue is raised in two of the contributions to this volume — those of Lengyel and of Martohardjono & Flynn respectively (Chapters 5 and 6). Lengyel, for instance, points to an apparent interaction between semantic and phonological factors in learners' attempts to pronounce novel lexis, which implies that L2 phonological events are differentially discerned and assimilated according to factors outside the strictly phonological domain. Martohardjono & Flynn, for their part, suggest that, as in the case of syntax, there may be certain aspects of second language phonological development (e.g. the recognition of some basic phonemic contrasts) that essentially reflect biologically endowed capacities, whereas others (e.g. the fine-tuning of accent) may be essentially data-driven. Obviously, if there are qualitatively diverse strands within the overall process of second language phonological development, then any age factor may affect each strand differently.

Finally in connection with second language phonological development, it behoves us to consider the *value* of investigating age in relation to second language accent acquisition. A very radical approach to this issue is that of Hill (1970) who calls into question the very reality of 'native accent'. She cites, for instance the case of South India, where large numbers of adults speak several local languages — Kannada, Tamil, etc. — and English too, using similar phonetic systems, and she suggests that in these circumstances distinguishing native from non-native accents may not be at all straightforward. In response to this point, one can, of course, easily reply that in other regions — Western Europe, for example — non-native accents do tend rather readily to be identified. However, such a response runs the risk of falling foul of the 'so what?' test. Cook (Chapter 2) expresses the view that, despite the attention it has received in second language age-related research, accent is the least important aspect of second language proficiency, and that older learners who fail to end up with a native-like accent lose little or nothing. Cook's opinion on this point will strike a chord with those who have criticised heavy doses of phonetic training in second language teaching using the argument that the only learners who really need to be able to pass themselves off as native speakers of the target language are trainee spies. On the other hand, it seems from the article by Bongaerts *et al.* (Chapter 1) that phonetic training can be efficacious. Moreover, common experience indicates that a poor accent can cause breakdowns in communication, and that even in less extreme cases it can induce a native speaker to 'switch off' during conversations and/or actually to seek to avoid further interactions with the learner in question. In this matter, we obviously need to find a *juste milieu* between overestimating and underestimating the importance of an authentic second language accent — always having regard to the particular communicative requirements of the learners concerned.

Age and the Second Language Lexicon

We come now to the question of age and the second language lexicon. This issue tends to have something of a Cinderella status in the whole debate about age and second language learning. Even as far as the present volume is concerned, while the lexicon is certainly discussed in some measure in a number of the contributions below, the age factor as it relates to second language lexical acquisition is not a matter that receives a great deal of attention. Given all of this, it may be worth exploring the evidence here and now in rather more detail in respect of lexis than has been attempted in respect of morphosyntax and phonology.

It has to be said at the outset that actually defining the domain of the lexicon — and in particular defining the line of demarcation between lexis and morphosyntax — is no easy matter. One notes in this connection that lexicographers constantly find themselves up against the problem of how best to display and integrate grammatical information relative to particular words in dictionary entries (see, e.g., Aarts, 1991; Carter, 1987: 128ff.; Cowie, 1983; Herbst, 1987; Lemmens & Wekker, 1991; Sinclair, 1987). This of itself already speaks volumes about the relationship between lexis and grammar. If dictionary makers, who, of all people, seek to plough a narrowly lexical furrow, are obliged to confront the treatment of morphosyntax, we must surely conclude that a partitioning-off of lexis from grammar is less than straightforward. The researches of computational lexicographers such as Gross (see, e.g., Gross, 1991) and his colleagues at the Laboratoire d'Automatique Documentaire et Linguistique very much confirm this view. It turns out that the principal theoretical problems which emerge from the construction of electronic lexica are 'essentiellement ceux de la séparation entre lexique et grammaire' (Gross, 1991: 107).

Moreover, descriptive and theoretical linguists in general have increasingly come to recognise the interaction between lexis and grammar. Within the philological tradition, for instance, Sandoz (1992) has been able to show that *-mentum* words in Latin evince a marked tendency to occur in a particular sentence position, namely in the predicate — a tendency he relates to the abstract quality of the meaning of such words. Within Chomskyan linguistics, to take another example, the interpenetration of the lexicon and morphosyntax is seen as twofold. On the one hand, lexis and highly specific language-particular grammatical features are lumped together as aspects of a given language that are outside the scope of operation of UG (see, e.g., Ioup, Martohardjono & Flynn, Chapters 4 and 6 respectively). On the other hand, the lexicon is also seen as interacting closely with UG-determined syntax. Indeed, a central principle of the 'Government and Binding' (GB) version of the Chomskyan model is the so-called 'Projection Principle', which states that 'the properties of lexical entries project onto the syntax of the sentence' (see Cook, 1988: 11; see also Cook's summary (Chapter 2) of relevant developments in more recent versions of the Chomskyan model).

In what follows in this section, the focus will be on aspects of language acquisition that are widely regarded as clearly lexical in nature: the learning of the forms and meanings of individual lexical items, the learning of 'local' grammar bound up with lexical choice (subcategorisation patterns, etc.), the learning of collocational restrictions, and so on. However, no definitive position is implied relative to the precise boundaries between lexis and morphosyntax, or indeed relative to the possibility that such boundaries may not actually exist.

Before homing in on the specifically second language dimension of age and lexical development, let us consider first language vocabulary acquisition, which represents the clearest possible demonstration of the fact that we continue to acquire language well beyond the childhood years and the clearest possible refutation of any notion that first language acquisition comes to a complete halt at any given maturational point (cf. Singleton, 1989: 54–9). We know that acquisition in this area continues well beyond the childhood years. For example, a number of researchers have written about the vast amount of new slang expressions that are taken on board in the teenage years and which serve to define group membership (see, e.g., Britton, 1970; Nelson & Rosenbaum, 1968; Schwartz & Merten, 1967). One can also in this context refer to the work of Smedts (1988) who, in a fairly large-scale study of first language word formation proficiency in Dutch between ages 7 and 17, found that his 7-year-old subjects displayed a mastery of just 14% of a range of Dutch word formation rules, that his

13-year-olds knew just 51% of the rules tested and that even his 17-year-olds demonstrated a command of only 66% of these rules. However, the continuation of first language lexical development clearly extends far beyond the teens. Indeed, it probably ends only when life ends. Carroll concludes (1971: 124) from his review of a number of lexical studies that first language vocabulary tends to increase significantly up to at least the age of 40 or 50, while Diller (1971: 29) reports research which suggests that there is no point before death at which vocabulary acquisition can be predicted to cease.

On the other hand, it does not seem to be the case that first language vocabulary learning proceeds in the same manner, at the same rate and level of efficiency throughout life. As far as vocabulary learning in adulthood is concerned, evidence from verbal memory research (see, e.g., Arenberg, 1983; Hussian, 1981: 6ff.) shows, for example, that the capacity of the elderly to recall memorised lexis in experimental conditions tends to be somewhat below that of younger subjects, especially in respect of speed of response — although, admittedly, there are always individuals whose performance is indistinguishable from that of their juniors. At the other end of the age-scale, it seems (see, e.g., M. Harris, 1992: 69ff.) that there are different periods in early language development associated with different kinds and rates of lexical development. The first three of these periods would appear to be: (i) a phase during which the child is endeavouring to discover what words are, how they can be used to refer, and what category or categories of entities particular words can be applied to; (ii) a 'vocabulary explosion' phase — after about 30 or more words have been learned — characterised by a very marked increase in the rate of lexical development; (iii) a phase beginning around age 3–4 which is marked by the revision, reorganisation and consolidation of lexical knowledge.

Turning now to the second language domain, there is no evidence, here either, of an age after which learning second language vocabulary becomes impossible. A recent study (Service, 1993; Service & Craik, 1993) examined the relative capacity of 20 young adults (mean age 25) and 20 older adults (mean age 72) to learn foreign-word equivalents for a list of unrelated words in their first language, English. The foreign items were either real Finnish words or pseudowords resembling English words. The results of this study clearly favoured the younger group in broad terms. However, the elderly subjects did not reveal themselves to be *incapable* of performing the task, and, indeed, some of them performed it reasonably well — particularly those who had had previous experience with word mnemonics and foreign languages (Service, personal communication). These results indicate in relation to second language development, just as other studies have shown in relation to first language development, that even senescence does not bring to an end the capacity to learn new words — even difficult new words — a finding which is broadly in line with the observations of those responsible for organising and teaching second language programmes for 'third-age' students (see, e.g., Brändle, 1986; cf. also Clyne, 1977).

With regard to second language vocabulary learning in the younger sector of the age spectrum, research findings appear on the whole to follow the pattern set by findings relative to age and the acquisition of morphosyntax. That is to say, short-term 'naturalistic' studies, all but one of the available short-term formal instructional studies, and all long-term formal instructional studies show adult and adolescent beginners progressing more rapidly than children in acquiring vocabulary, and older children progressing more rapidly than younger children. On the other hand, as far as long-term outcomes are concerned, 'naturalistic' studies suggest that, in lexis as in other areas, the younger one starts the higher the level of proficiency one is likely eventually to attain.

Amongst the pertinent short-term naturalistic studies, one can cite Ekstrand's (1976) investigation of the proficiency in Swedish of 2189 immigrant children of school age in Sweden, the median of whose length of exposure to Swedish was 10.5 months. Tests for pronunciation transcription from dictation, listening comprehension, reading comprehension, free oral production and free written production were administered to these subjects (or, in the case of pronunciation and free oral production tests, to subsamples thereof), and all test results were found to correlate positively and significantly with age. There was, admittedly, in the array of tests used in this study no instrument focusing solely on lexis, but the comprehension tests and production tests, which set the tasks of, respectively, matching descriptions to and formulating descriptions of pictures, relied very heavily on lexical knowledge. Also relevant in this connection are the studies of Snow & Hoefnagel-Höhle (1978a, 1978b), referred to above, which show adult and adolescent naturalistic learners of Dutch outperforming younger beginners in the short term in their command of Dutch lexis — as in other domains — but beginning to fall behind their juniors after about a year. Lexical competence in this case was gauged by a version of the Peabody Picture Vocabulary Test.

Of the short-duration formal instruction-based experiments which have a bearing in the present context, a much-quoted example is Asher & Price's (1967) investigation. This involved subjects distributed across four different age-groups (adults, eighth-graders, fourth-graders and second-graders) in three short training sessions in respect of simple commands in Russian, a language in which none had had any previous experience. In retention tests, which were in very large measure focused on the communicative import of the lexis in question, performance was found *grosso modo* to be positively correlated with maturity — i.e. the older the age-group the better its overall results. Another short-term school-based study which is of interest, is the earlier-mentioned investigation by Ekstrand (1978) of 1,000+ Swedish pupils ranging in age from 8 to 11 who had been exposed to 18 weeks of instruction in English. The tests administered to these subjects included an English–Swedish translation task based on oral stimuli, the completion of which clearly depended principally on phonologically accessed lexical knowledge. This test, as well as all the other tests deployed by Ekstrand, yielded results which improved more or less linearly with age. A third, less well-known, instance of a partly lexically focused study conducted in a formal instructional environment is that of Stankowski Gratton (1980). This investigated a younger and an older group of Italian primary-school pupils (average age 6 and 8, respectively) following a beginners' course in German over a school year. The final test, half of which was lexis-centred, and all of which was oral–aural in nature, revealed the older group as having a substantial lead over the younger group, these results coinciding with impressions recorded during observation of the two groups in class.

The one study which runs against the general trend in seeming to indicate an *immediate* vocabulary-learning advantage for younger L2 beginners is that of Yamada, Takasuka, Kotake & Kurusu (1980). The subjects for this study were 30 Japanese elementary school pupils, all of average academic achievement, distributed evenly across three age-groups (ten 7-year-olds, ten 9-year-olds, ten 11-year-olds). The experiment investigated the success of these subjects, none of whom had had any previous experience of English, at learning a small selection of English words. From a list of 40 English mono- and di-syllabic words, the denotatum of each of which was represented in an associated picture, each subject was given four items to learn, along with the corresponding pictures, in two sessions separated by 24 hours. In individual tests it was found that mean learning scores decreased with age. The inconsistency of these findings with those of other studies involving instructed learners could perhaps be connected with the highly limited, extremely artificial, entirely decontextualised nature of the learning task in question. In any case, the clear trend of results from most studies is for younger children to perform less well in the short term.

In relation to long-term school-based studies, one of the studies referred to earlier in a general context, that of Oller & Nagato (1974) will serve very well to illustrate the lexical dimension of the issue at hand. They looked at 233 Japanese learners of English as a second language from the seventh, ninth and eleventh grades of a private elementary and secondary school system for girls, and at each grade included some pupils who had experienced six years of early instruction in English and some pupils who had not. These learners had administered to them a 50-item English cloze-test, a separate test having been constructed for each grade-level. Oller & Nagato summarise the test results as follows:

> The first comparison shows a highly significant difference between FLES and non-FLES students at the seventh grade level. This difference is reduced by the ninth grade though still significant; at the eleventh grade it is insignificant. (Oller & Nagato, 1974: 18)

They take their findings as evidence against the claim that early L2 instruction yields long-term benefits, the obvious implication of the results being that older beginners can assimilate as much in five years as younger beginners can in eleven. The relevance of these findings to second language lexical development derives from the fact that proficiency in this case was gauged using cloze-tests, which essentially require the deployment of various kinds of lexical and lexically-related knowledge (cf. comments below regarding C-test data).

As far as evidence from long-term naturalistic studies is concerned, one can mention two relatively recent long-term Swedish studies, conducted by Mägiste (1987) and Hyltenstam (1988, 1992) respectively. Using a cross-sectional research design, Mägiste (1987) tested the capacity of 151 young native speakers of German (77 high school students and 74 elementary school students) who had been resident in Sweden for various lengths of time to name pictured objects and two-digit numbers in German and Swedish. She found that the point at which the response times for naming objects in the two languages intersected occurred after four years' residence as far as the elementary school sample was concerned but only after six years' residence in the high school group — from which she infers an advantage for the younger group in terms of the acquisition of elementary second language lexis. With regard to the naming of two-digit numbers, the two groups' response times for Swedish coincided with their response times for German at about the same point, namely after three to four years. Mägiste's comment on this latter result is that 'it is remarkable that the elementary school students achieved the point of language balance at the same time as the high school pupils, despite the fact this task was more difficult for the younger students', the implication seeming to be that the younger learners' lexis-acquiring advantage compensated for their general cognitive disadvantage.

Hyltenstam (1988, 1992) studied two groups of subjects, of Finnish-speaking and Spanish-speaking backgrounds respectively, who had migrated to Sweden before (in one case during) puberty and whose period of residence in Sweden exceeded five years (except in one case where the length of residence was three years). Swedish data, both oral and written, were elicited from these subjects, and similar data were obtained from a control group of Swedish native speakers. When all subjects' errors, both grammatical and lexical, were analysed it became clear that the numbers of errors produced by subjects who had arrived in Sweden after age 7 were consistently in a higher range than the numbers of errors produced by the native speakers, whereas the range of numbers of errors produced by subjects who had arrived in Sweden before age 6 overlapped with those of the other two groups.

The pattern presented above is confirmed by a the results obtained in a study conducted by the present author (Singleton, 1992b, 1993) within the framework of the Trinity College Dublin Modern Languages Project. The results in question are based on an analysis of French C-test data. C-tests are, like cloze-tests, reduced redundancy procedures, but in the case of C-tests what is involved is the restoration to wholeness of texts in which, after an initial lead-in passage, the second half of every second word has been deleted. Since subjects taking a test of this kind are unable to manipulate the ordering of units in the text, the knowledge that is probed is for the most part clearly lexical in nature — knowledge of content words, grammatical words, collocability, subcategorisation frames, etc.

The C-test data in question were elicited in 1990–91 and 1991–92 from two groups of English-speaking formal learners of French — 10 from the 1990–91 intake and 10 from the 1991–92 intake of first-year students of French at Trinity College Dublin, both groups having been selected from larger sets of volunteers. One of the criteria for the composition of the groups was that each group should contain subjects who had begun learning French at an early age as well as later beginners. The volunteers from the 1990–91 intake had all begun French relatively late. Accordingly, the range of beginning ages represented in the 1990–91 group (henceforth Group A) is relatively narrow (10–12 years). The 1991–92 volunteers, on the other hand, had first encountered French at a wide variety of ages (from age 3 to age 12), and this is reflected in the group of subjects selected from this cohort (henceforth Group B).

French C-test data elicited from each group were organised into two batches: those emanating from subjects who began learning French before age 12 and those emanating from subjects who began learning the language beyond age 12. Age 12 was chosen as the dividing line because it tends to coincide with the onset of puberty, which has traditionally been taken as the end point of the critical period for language learning, and because certain researchers (e.g. Long, 1990) specifically refer to it as crucial in this connection. Because there was no possibility of separating out the age variable from the length of exposure variable, it was recognised that any advantage found for earlier beginners could not be taken as clear evidence of an age factor at work, but would have to be seen as merely suggestive. Superior or equal performance from later beginners, on the other hand, could not but be interpreted as indicating faster L2 vocabulary learning on their part at least at the current stage of the process.

The mean scores for the under-12 beginners and the 12+ beginners from Group A (Table 1) revealed neither subset to be consistently ahead of the other in terms of these scores. Moreover, in no case did the difference between the scores obtained by the two subsets attain statistical significance. Thus it appears that the lexical proficiency of those subjects in this group who had started French before age 12 did not surpass that of those

Table 1 Mean C-test scores obtained by Group A subjects who had begun French before age 12 and beyond age 12 respectively (maximum possible score = 50)

	December 1990		*May 1991*	
	C-test 1	C-test 2	C-test 3	C-test 4
Under-12 beginners	*N* = 6		*N* = 6	
	41.0	38.2	42.7	36.8
12+ beginners	*N* = 4		*N* = 4	
	39.5	36.0	42.8	38.0
	December 1991		*May 1992*	
	C-test 1	C-test 2	C-test 3	C-test 4
Under12 beginners	*N* = 6		*N* = 6	
	41.3	41.5	42.8	37.4
12+ beginners	*N* = 4		*N* = 4	
	43.0	40.0	44.3	41.0

Table 2 Mean C-test scores obtained by Group B subjects who had begun French before age 12 and beyond age 12 respectively (maximum score = 50)

	December 1991		*May 1991*	
	C-test 1	C-test 2	C-test 3	C-test 4
Under-12 beginners	*N* = 7		*N* = 5	
	38.7	32.4	39.6	34.2
12+ beginners	*N* = 3		*N* = 3	
	30.3	27.0	33.3	26.0

who began French beyond age 12 in spite of the former's extra exposure to the language. This finding is in line what emerges from the majority of the above-discussed research on the outcome of early second language lexical learning in formal instructional situations.

The (for obvious reasons sparser) results from Group B (Table 2) present a rather different picture from that which emerges from the Group A results, in the sense that the under-12 beginners consistently outscored the 12+ beginners — all differences between the two sets of scores attaining significance at (at least) the $p < 0.1$ level on a one-tailed test.

Given that Group B contained some somewhat earlier beginners than Group A, the difference between the Group B results and the Group A results looks like good news for those such as Long (1990, personal communication) and Hyltenstam (1988, 1992) who, while accepting the onset of puberty as the upper limit for a critical or sensitive period for L2 learning, incline to the view that the chances of a child beginner achieving native-like competence in an L2 diminish progressively from age 6 onwards. To refer back to the point made above, however, it must be remembered that the earlier learning started the longer it had been going on, so that any advantage that might be attributed to an age factor is equally attributable to a length of exposure factor. What may have been at work here, in fact, was an interaction between the age factor and the length of exposure factor, in the sense that the longer learning had been under way the more time the long-term advantage of an early start had had to begin to manifest itself and to emerge from the masking effect of later beginners' initial advantage. On the other hand, whatever the relationship between age of starting to learn the L2 and eventual outcome, it is obviously not a simple or an absolute one; thus, within Group B it is by no means consistently the case that the earlier learning started the better the performance recorded, as can be seen from Table 3, which details

Table 3 Individual Group B C-test scores in relation to age at which learning of French commenced (maximum score = 50)

Score	*C-test 1 Age*	*C-test 2 Age*	*C-test 3 Age*	*C-test 4 Age*
47			8	
44	8	8		8
42			11	
41	3			
39	8			
	11			
38	7		3	
			11	
37	11			11
36		7		
35			12	
			12	
34				3
33	6	3	8	
	12			
32	12	8		
31				12
30		11	12	
29				8
28		12		
27	12	6		11
		12		
26		12		
25		11		12
22				12

individual Group B scores by age of first instructional encounter with French.

Another aspect of the C-test results that was considered by Singleton (1992b, 1993) was whether the earlier beginners showed greater improvement over time than the later beginners. It was possible to examine this question at the time of the study only in relation to Group A, since only this group had at that stage taken particular tests twice — with a 12-month interval. A comparison of this group's 1990 and 1991 scores revealed that both subsets of the group scored better in 1991 than in 1990, and that the improvements recorded were statistically significant in every case except one (this involving the younger beginners). There was no evidence here, therefore, of an earlier start in formal L2 instruction leading to more rapid L2 lexical development at the advanced study stage.

Finally, with regard to the *kinds* of lexical errors produced by the two subsets of subjects in each group it did not appear to be the case that subjects who began French after age 12 produced significantly higher numbers of errors in particular categories than those who had an earlier start. Thus, for example, whereas it might have been speculated that subjects who started learning French around puberty might have a tendency to produce more lexical innovations — i.e. forms that do not actually exist in French — than the earlier starters, in fact there was no significant trend in this direction (Tables 4 and 5).

In sum, there is no evidence with regard to second language learning any more than with regard to first language learning that the capacity to acquire new vocabulary disappears at any particular maturational point, or that it necessarily becomes radically impaired even in old age. It appears from the relatively small amount of available published research on the topic that the age factor operates in relation to second language vocabulary learning in the same way as it operates in relation to other aspects of second language learning, i.e. older beginners exhibit an initial advantage which is progressively eroded as younger beginners catch up with them and eventually overtake them. This pattern is clear in the naturalistic evidence, and is undisturbed by most of the evidence from formal instructional situations, provided that one takes into account the very much longer timescale that must be required for the eventual advantage of an early start to manifest itself under conditions of sparse exposure. As far as the Trinity College Dublin Modern Languages Research Project results reported here are concerned, these are entirely compatible with the view of the role of age in second language vocabulary learning that has already been set out; the one aspect of the results that appears to offer prospects of breaking new

Table 4 Proportions of non-scoring slots accounted for by lexically innovative errors in the C-test performances of Group A subjects who began French before and beyond age 12 respectively

	December 1991		*May 1991*	
	C-test 1	*C-test 2*	*C-test 3*	*C-test 4*
Under-12 beginners	$N = 6$		$N = 6$	
	0.37	0.31	0.19	0.16
12+ beginners	$N = 4$		$N = 4$	
	0.44	0.25	0.14	0.22
	December 1991		*May 1992*	
	C-test 1	*C-test 2*	*C-test 3*	*C-test 4*
Under-12 beginners	$N = 6$		$N = 6$	
	0.36	0.31	0.22	0.21
Under+ beginners	$N = 4$		$N = 4$	
	0.25	0.23	0.18	0.22

Table 5 Proportions of non-scoring slots accounted for by lexically innovative errors in the C-test performances of Group B subjects who began French before and beyond age 12 respectively

	December 1991		*May 1991*	
	C-test 1	C-test 2	C-test 3	C-test 4
Under-12 beginners	$N = 7$		$N = 5$	
	0.38	0.23	0.13	0.14
12+ beginners	$N = 3$		$N = 3$	
	0.40	0.25	0.20	0.08

ground is the indication that a subsample containing some very early beginners is exhibiting a degree of second language lexical proficiency which significantly surpasses that of a subsample of subjects who started learning the second language at 12+ — a finding which, if replicated as the Project proceeds, may at last begin to offer some concrete and quantifiable evidence of the long-term benefits of foreign language learning in the primary school.

Again, however, it must be stressed that the above-noted tendency for younger learners to do better in the long run in the matter of second language lexical acquisition is no more than a tendency. We have seen with regard to the Trinity College Dublin Modern Languages Research Project results that within any age-cohort there can be wide variation in terms of second language lexical proficiency levels eventually attained. Moreover, the remarks made earlier about the need to bear in mind that syntactic acquisition and phonological acquisition may not be monolithic processes also apply in the case of lexical acquisition. Indeed they would seem to apply *a fortiori* in the case of lexical acquisition, given the multidimensionality of the lexicon — the fact that, so to speak, it has its fingers in every part not only of the linguistic pie but of the cognitive pie generally. If, as has been suggested by some (see above), different aspects of second language syntax and phonology are differentially affected by age, then we must expect differential effects too in respect of different aspects of the second language lexicon.

The Contributions to this Volume

Reference has already been made in various parts of the foregoing discussion to the contributions which form the basis of the chapters that follow. In this final section of the Introduction it is appropriate to provide a little more information about the content of these chapters.

In Chapter 1 Bongaerts, Planken & Schils address the question of accent acquisition in a second language at the end of the critical period as commonly defined (around age 12). Their findings indicate that, at least for Dutch learners of English, such a relatively late start does not preclude the possibility of acquiring a pronunciation in the second language which is indistinguishable from that of native speakers — at least as judged by the native speaker ear. Bongaerts *et al.* emphasise in their discussion of their results the fact that Dutch and English are closely related typologically (cf. Kellerman's observations cited above) and also the fact that their successful accent-acquirers were university students majoring in English who had received special training in phonetics/phonology besides large amounts of unstructured oral input. They interpret their findings as suggesting a variation on Long's 1983 title, namely that 'Instruction in the pronunciation of a second language does make a difference'. This conclusion will come as no surprise to phoneticians, but may well raise some eyebrows in other quarters.

Cook's contribution, which constitutes Chapter 2, explores his notion of multicompetence in relation to the Critical Period Hypothesis. Much of this article is devoted to critiquing the idea that second language learners who do not achieve monolingual native speaker competence in their target language should be regarded as failures, his argument being that the competence of a person knowing more than one language is qualitatively different from that of the monolingual, so that monolingual competence is quite simply an inappropriate yardstick. Cook also discusses the issue of the extent to which the language systems present in the bilingual's mind are developed and maintained separately or in an integrated manner, suggesting that the age at which acquisition begins may have a role in determining the degree of separation/integration involved. His provisional conclusion from a review of the relevant research is that, after an initial semantically organised phase, child bilinguals tend to keep the two language systems distinct, whereas bilingualism beginning in adulthood may be characterised by a unitary system, at least as far as vocabulary is concerned. He goes on to argue that his multicompetence model is not threatened by evidence of some degree of separation of the language systems in question, any more than the existence of style-shifting within a given language undermines the essential integrity of competence in that language. He ends by relating his discussion of separation and integration in bilingual competence to recent developments in Chomskyan theory.

In Chapter 3, Penfield's part in the evolution of thinking about age and second language learning is closely scrutinised by Dechert. Dechert's thesis is that two important metaphors deployed by Penfield in the making of claims in respect of his 'optimum age' hypothesis are inadequate and unhelpful. Dechert notes that part of Penfield's argument is that the pre-linguistic brain is a 'clean slate' on which nothing has been written and that language acquisition subsequently leads to an irreversible functional fixation. Dechert suggests that this *tabula rasa* metaphor can be connected to Penfield's visit to the Iraq Museum, which by his own account made a deep impression on him, and during which he was shown clay tablets inscribed with Sumerian pictographs. Penfield's speculations on language learning during the period of Babylonian domination of Sumer, as well as his reflections on the image of the 'soft clay tablet', were, Dechert claims, important — but fundamentally unscientific — elements in his espousal of the *tabula rasa* metaphor. The second Penfieldian metaphor dealt with by Dechert is that of 'unit'. Dechert shows that Penfield's conception of the units of language processing — a prominent *leitmotiv* in his discussion of 'speech mechanisms' and language learning — is simplistic and obscure.

Chapter 4 is a wide-ranging report by Ioup on some of the research she has been conducting with two subjects who learned Arabic as a second language in their adult years in an Arabic-speaking environment. The question raised by Ioup is whether input enhancement is essential in order for adult second language learners to attain native-like levels of proficiency in their target language. She compares the performance of her two subjects, one of whom is entirely untutored in Arabic and the other of whom received extensive formal instruction, on a range of tasks — speech production, accent identification, translation, grammaticality judgment and interpretation of anaphora. It transpires that the differences between these two learners are marginal, both attaining levels of performance close to native norms. This prompts Ioup to consider the hypothesis that for those few second language learners who are able to achieve native-like proficiency formal instruction may not be a prerequisite. However, she treats this hypothesis with caution, observing that her untutored subject in fact engaged in a certain amount of self-tuition through the taking and continual revision of notes about the grammar, lexis and phonology of Arabic and that she welcomed and exploited the negative evidence provided by corrective feedback.

Chapter 5, like Chapter 1, is firmly focused on phonetics and phonology. In this chapter Lengyel challenges the notion that children are better equipped than adults to acquire native-like accents in foreign languages. He points to the difficulty of coming to a universally valid conclusion on this matter in the light of the complexity of cross-linguistic phonological relationships. He also suggests that language teachers' practical experience does not support the claim that children are necessarily adept at accent acquisition, and argues that individual learning strategies will inevitably lead to individual variation in quality of accent. He then presents two sets of experimental results which on the on hand call into question Scovel's (1988) claim that foreign-accent recognition develops as the critical period ends (around 10–12 years), and on the other indicate that young children's capacity to repeat foreign words accurately is distinctly limited. For Lengyel both sets of results cast doubt on what he sees as simplistic assumptions about the phonological dimension of the age factor in second language acquisition.

Finally, in Chapter 6, Martohardjono & Flynn, basing themselves broadly on the Chomskyan paradigm, make a sharp distinction between those aspects of second language proficiency which in terms of the Chomskyan approach can be seen as 'biologically endowed' and those aspects which may be considered to lie outside the innate language faculty and thus to be subject to developmental vicissitudes. They apply this distinction to both syntax acquisition and to the acquisition of sound systems, and they argue that, whereas the non-innate aspects may well be susceptible to age-related effects, the innate aspects are likely to be immune to such effects, essentially remaining fully available to the adult language learner. They review a range of research, including research which they themselves have carried out, and come to the conclusion that the distinction they propose is validated by such research. They further suggest that such a distinction makes a useful contribution to the provision of an explanation for some of the apparent contradictions discernible in the literature in this area.

References

AARTS, F. 1991, OALD, LDOCE and COBUILD: Three dictionaries of English compared. In GRANGER (ed.) (pp. 211–26).

ARENBERG, D. 1983, Memory and learning do decline late in life. In J. BIRREN, H. THOMAE and M. MAROIS (eds) *Aging: A Challenge to Science and Society. Volume 3. Behavioural Sciences and Conclusions* (pp. 312–22). Oxford: Oxford University Press.

ASHER, J. and GARCÍA, G. 1969, The optimal age to learn a foreign language. *Modern Language Journal* 38, 334–41. Reprinted in KRASHEN, SCARCELLA and LONG (eds) (1982) (pp. 3–12).

ASHER, J. and PRICE, B. 1967, The learning strategy of the Total Physical Response: Some age differences. *Child Development* 38, 1219–27. Reprinted in KRASHEN, SCARCELLA and LONG (eds) (1982) (pp. 76–83).

BLEY-VROMAN, R. 1994, Updating the Fundamental Difference Hypothesis. Paper presented at the Fourth Annual Conference of the European Second Language Association (EUROSLA). Aix-en-Provence. Abstract in *EUROSLA 4: Abstracts* (pp. 6–7).

BRÄNDLE, M. 1986, Language teaching for the 'young-old'. *Babel* 21, 17–21.

BREATHNACH, C. 1993, Temporal determinants of language acquisition and bilingualism. *Irish Journal of Psychological Medicine* 10 (1), 41–7.

BRITTON, J. 1970, *Language and Learning*. Harmondsworth: Penguin.

BURSTALL, C., JAMIESON, M., COHEN, S. and HARGREAVES, M. 1974, *Primary French in the Balance*. Windsor: NFER Publishing Company.

CARROLL, J. 1971, Development of native language skills beyond the early years. In C. REED (ed.) *The Learning of Language* (pp. 97–156). New York: Appleton-Century-Crofts.

CARTER, R. 1987, *Vocabulary: Applied Linguistic Perspectives*. London: Allen and Unwin.

CMIEB/CLA/Ville de Besançon 1992, *Actes de la IVe Rencontre Internationale Langues et Cités. L'enseignement précoce des langues en Europe à l'horizon 2000: bilan et perspectives.* Besançon: Centre Mondial d'Information sur l'Education Bilingue/Centre de Linguistique Appliquée/Ville de Besançon.

CLYNE, M. 1977, Bilingualism of the elderly. *Talanya* 4, 45–56.

COOK, V. 1988, *Chomsky's Universal Grammar: An Introduction*. Oxford: Blackwell.

— 1991, *Second Language Learning and Language Teaching*. London: Edward Arnold.

COWIE, A. 1983, On specifying grammar. In R. Hartmann (ed.) *Lexicography: Principles and Practice* (pp. 99–107) . London: Academic Press.
DABÈNE, L. 1990, Pour une didactique de la variation. In L. DABÈNE, F. CICUREL, M.-C. LAUGA-HAMID and C. FOERSTER (eds) *Variations et rituels en classe de langue* (pp.7–21). Paris: Hatier-CRÉDIF.
DILLER, K. 1971, *Generative Grammar, Structural Linguistics and Language Teaching*. Rowley, MA: Newbury House.
DUNKEL, H. and PILLET, R. 1957, A second year of French in the elementary school. *Elementary School Journal* 58, 142–51.
EKSTRAND, L. 1976, Age and length of residence as variables related to the adjustment of migrant children, with special reference to second language learning. In G. NICKEL (ed.) *Proceedings of the Fourth International Congress of Applied Linguistics. Volume 3* (pp. 179–97). Stuttgart: Hochschulverlag. Reprinted in KRASHEN, SCARCELLA and LONG (eds) (1982) (pp. 123–35).
— 1978, English without a book revisited: The effect of age on second language acquisition in a formal setting. *Didakometry* 60, Department of Educational and Psychological Research, School of Education, Malmö. Reprinted in KRASHEN, SCARCELLA and LONG (eds) (1982) (pp. 136–58).
ELLIS, R. 1994, *The Study of Second Language Acquisition*. Oxford: Oxford University Press.
ERVIN-TRIPP, S. 1974, Is second language learning like the first? *TESOL Quarterly* 8, 111–27.
EUROSLA 1994, *EUROSLA 4: Abstracts*. Aix-en-Provence: Université de Provence.
FATHMAN, A. 1975, The relationship between age and second language productive ability. *Language Learning* 25, 245–53. Reprinted in KRASHEN, SCARCELLA and LONG (eds) (1982) (pp. 115–122).
GRANGER, S. (ed.) 1991, *Perspectives on the English Lexicon: A Tribute to Jacques van Roey*. Louvain-la-Neuve: Institut de Linguistique (*Cahiers de l'Institut de Linguistique de Louvain* 17 (1–3)).
GROSS, M. 1991, Lexique et syntaxe, *Travaux de Linguistique* 23, 107–132.
HARLEY, B. 1986, *Age in Second Language Acquisition*. Clevedon: Multilingual Matters.
HARRIS, J. 1992, Foreign languages in primary schools: Weighing the evidence. *Teangeolas: Iris Institiúid Teangeolaíochta Éireann/Journal of the Linguistics Institute of Ireland* 30/31, 15–27.
HARRIS, M. 1992, *Language Experience and Early Language Development: From Input to Uptake*. Hove: Lawrence Erlbaum.
HERBST, T. 1987, A proposal for a valency grammar of English. In R. ILSON (ed.) *A Spectrum of Lexicography* (pp. 29–47). Amsterdam: John Benjamins.
HILL, J. 1970, Foreign accents, language acquisition and cerebral dominance revisited. *Language Learning* 20, 237–48.
HUSSIAN, R. 1981, *Geriatric Psychology: A Behavioral Perspective*. New York: Van Nostrand Reinhold.
HYLTENSTAM, K. 1988, Att tala svenska som en infödd — eller nästan. In K. HYLTENSTAM, K. and I. LINDBERG (eds) *Första symposiet om svenska som andraspråk. Volym I: Föredrag om språk, språkinlärning och interaktion* (pp. 138–56). Stockholm: Centrum för tvåspråkighetsforskning.

— 1992, Non-native features of near-native speakers: On the ultimate attainment of childhood L2 learners. In R. HARRIS (ed.) *Cognitive Processing in Bilinguals* (pp. 351–68). Amsterdam: Elsevier.
JOHNSON, J. 1992, Critical period effects in second language acquisition: The effect of written versus auditory materials on the assessment of grammatical competence. *Language Learning* 42, 217–48.
JOHNSON, J. and NEWPORT, E. 1989, Critical period effects in second language learning: The influence of maturational state on the acquisition of ESL. *Cognitive Psychology* 21, 60–99.
JOHNSTONE, R. 1991, Foreign language in primary schools: Evaluating the National Pilot Projects in Scotland. *Language Learning Journal* 4, 36–8.
KELLERMAN, E. forthcoming, Age before beauty: Johnson and Newport revisited. To appear in L. EUBANK, L. SELINKER and M. SHARWOOD SMITH (eds) *Festschrift for Bill Rutherford*. Amsterdam: John Benjamins.
KESSLER, C and IDAR, I. 1979, Acquisition of English by a Vietnamese mother and child. *Working Papers on Bilingualism* 18, 65–79.
KRASHEN, S., LONG, M. and SCARCELLA, R. 1979, Age, rate and eventual attainment in second language acquisition. *TESOL Quarterly* 13, 573–82. Reprinted in KRASHEN, SCARCELLA and LONG (eds) (1982) (pp. 161–72).
KRASHEN, S., SCARCELLA, R. and LONG, M. (eds) 1982, *Child–Adult Differences in Second Language Acquisition*. Rowley, MA: Newbury House.
LEMMENS, M. and WEKKER, H. 1991, On the relationship between lexis and grammar in English learners' dictionaries. In GRANGER (ed.) (pp. 227–42).
LENNEBERG, E. 1967, *Biological Foundations of Language*. New York: Wiley.
LONG, M. 1983, Does second language instruction make a difference? A review of the research. *TESOL Quarterly* 17, 359–82.
— 1990, Maturational constraints on language development. *Studies in Second Language Acquisition* 12, 251–85.
MÄGISTE, E. 1987, Further evidence for the optimal age hypothesis in second language learning. In J. LANTOLF and A. LABARCA (eds) *Language Learning: Focus on the Classroom* (pp. 51–8). Norwood, NJ: Ablex.
NELSON, E. and ROSENBAUM, E. 1968, Sociolinguistic dimensions of youth culture. Paper presented at the the meeting of the American Educational Research Association. Chicago.
OLLER, J. and NAGATO, N. 1974, The long-term effect of FLES: An experiment. *Modern Language Journal* 58, 15–19.
OLSON, L. and SAMUELS, S. 1973, The relationship between age and accuracy of foreign language pronunciation. *Journal of Educational Research* 66, 263–67. Reprinted in KRASHEN, SCARCELLA and LONG (eds) (1982) (pp. 67–75).
PATKOWSKI, M. 1980, The sensitive period for the acquisition of syntax in a second language. *Language Learning* 30, 449–72.
PENFIELD, W. and ROBERTS, L. 1959, *Speech and Brain Mechanisms*. Princeton, NJ: Princeton University Press.
PINCEMIN, J. and O'NEIL, C. (eds) 1990, *Langues, cultures et systèmes éducatifs: enjeux de la construction de l'Europe*. Lille: Arpeij, and Paris: Université de Paris III.
ROMAINE, S. 1989, *Bilingualism*. Oxford: Blackwell.

SANDOZ, C. (1992). Syntaxe et formation des mots: un type d'emploi de noms verbaux en latin, *TRANEL* 18 (Institut de Linguistique, Université de Neuchâtel), 245–52.

SCHWARTZ, G. and MERTEN, D. 1967, The language of adolescence: An anthropological approach to the youth culture. *The American Journal of Anthropology* 72, 453–68.

SCOVEL, T. 1988, *A Time to Speak. A Psycholinguistic Inquiry into the Critical Period for Human Speech*. Rowley, MA: Newbury House.

SELIGER, H., KRASHEN, S. and LADEFOGED, P. 1975, Maturational constraints in the acquisition of second languages. *Language Sciences* 38, 20–2. Reprinted in KRASHEN, SCARCELLA and LONG (eds) (1982) (pp. 13–19).

SERVICE, E. 1993, Phonological and semantic aspects of memory for foreign language. In J. CHAPELLE and M.-T. CLAES (eds) *Actes: 1er Congrès International: Mémoire et Mémorisation dans l'Acquisition et l'Apprentissage des Langues. Proceedings: 1st International Congress: Memory and Memorization in Acquiring and Learning Languages* (pp. 307–17). Louvain-la-Neuve: CLL.

SERVICE, E. and CRAIK, F. 1993, Differences between young and older adults in learning a foreign language. *Journal of Memory and Language* 32, 608–23.

SINCLAIR, J. 1987, Grammar in the dictionary. In J. SINCLAIR (ed.) *Looking Up: An Account of the COBUILD Project in Lexical Computing and the Development of the Collins COBUILD English Language Dictionary* (pp. 104–15). London: Collins.

SINGLETON, D. 1981, *Age as a Factor in Second Language Acquisition: A Review of Some Recent Research*. Dublin: Trinity College, Centre for Language and Communication Studies (CLCS Occasional Paper 3). ERIC ED 217 712.

— 1989, *Language Acquisition: The Age Factor*. Clevedon: Multilingual Matters.

— 1992a, Second language instruction: The when and the how. *AILA Review* 9, 46–54.

— 1992b, Age and the L2 lexicon. Paper presented at the Fourteenth Annual Meeting of the American Association for Applied Linguistics. Seattle.

— 1993, Exploring the L2 mental lexicon. Paper presented at the Third Annual Conference of the European Second Language Association (EUROSLA). Sofia.

SMEDTS, W. 1988, De beheersing van de nederlandse woordvorming tussen 7 en 17. In F. VAN BESIEN (ed.) *First Language Acquisition* (pp. 103–27). Antwerp: Association Belge de Linguistique Appliquée/Universitaire Instelling Antwerpen (*ABLA Papers* No. 12).

SNOW, C. and HOEFNAGEL-HÖHLE, M. 1977, Age differences in the pronunciation of foreign sounds. *Language and Speech* 20, 357–65. Reprinted in KRASHEN, SCARCELLA and LONG (eds) (1982) (pp. 84–92).

— 1978a, Age differences in second language acquisition. In G. NICKEL (ed.) *Applied Linguistics. Psycholinguistics* (pp. 293–309). Stuttgart: Hochschulverlag.

— 1978b, The critical period for language acquisition: Evidence from second language learning. *Child Development* 49, 1114–28. Reprinted in KRASHEN, SCARCELLA and LONG (eds) (1982) (pp. 93–111).

STANKOWSKI GRATTON, R. 1980, Una ricerca sperimentale sull'insegnamento del tedesco dalla prima classe elementare. *Rassegna Italiana di Linguistica Applicata* 12 (3), 119–41.

STENGEL, E. 1939, On learning a new language. *International Journal of Psychoanalysis* 20, 471–79.

STERN, H. 1976, Optimal age: Myth or reality? *Canadian Modern Language Review* 32, 283–94.

TAHTA, S., WOOD, M. and LOEWENTHAL, K. 1981, Age changes in the ability to replicate foreign pronunciation and intonation. *Language and Speech* 24, 363–72.

TITONE, R. 1986, Un passaporto per il futuro. *L'Educatore* 34 (6), 4–9.

TOMB, J. (1925). On the intuitive capacity of children to understand spoken languages. *British Journal of Psychology* 16, 53–4.

VAN WUIJTSWINKEL, K. 1994, Critical period effects on the acquisition of grammatical competence in a second language. BA thesis. Department of Applied Linguistics, Nijmegen University.

VILKE, M. and VRHOVAC, Y. (eds) 1993, *Children and Foreign Languages/Les enfants et les langues étrangères*. Zagreb: Faculty of Philosophy, University of Zagreb.

YAMADA, J., TAKASUTA, S., KOTAKE, N. and KURUSU, J. 1980, On the optimum age for teaching foreign language vocabulary to children. *International Review of Applied Linguistics in Language Teaching* 18, 245–47.

1 Can Late Starters Attain a Native Accent in a Foreign Language? A Test of the Critical Period Hypothesis

THEO BONGAERTS, BRIGITTE PLANKEN and ERIK SCHILS

Introduction

It is a commonly held belief that, compared to adults, children are very successful second language learners. After settling in another language community, children seem to pick up the new language without much effort, whereas their parents experience great difficulty in achieving high levels of L2 proficiency. This seems to be particularly true for the acquisition of accent: it has been claimed that there are exceptional cases of adult learners who, like young learners, have attained native levels of proficiency in a second language with regard to vocabulary, morphology and syntax, but who still speak it with a noticeable foreign accent. A much-quoted example in this respect is Joseph Conrad, the Polish-born author of English novels, whose books are required reading for students of English literature. Conrad learned English as a third language after childhood and, while becoming a fluent and creative writer in that language, continued to speak it with a strong Polish accent. In his honour, Scovel (1981, 1988) has called the mismatch between lexical, morphological and syntactic performance and pronunciation the 'Joseph Conrad phenomenon'. Another well-known example is the former US Secretary of State Henry Kissinger, whose pronunciation of English immediately betrays his German origin (Brown, 1987).

The phenomenon of children seeming to have the edge over adults when it comes to language learning has led to the hypothesis that there is an *optimal age* (Penfield, 1963; Asher & García, 1969), a *sensitive period* (Oyama, 1976) or a *critical period* (Lenneberg, 1967; Scovel, 1988) for second language acquisition. According to the *Critical Period Hypothesis*, which is usually associated with the name of Lenneberg, there is a biologically — or more specifically a neurologically — based period, ending around age 12, at the onset of puberty, beyond which complete mastery of a second language is no longer possible. In *Biological Foundations of Language*, published in 1967, Lenneberg placed much emphasis on the relationship between language acquisition and the progressive specialisation of the cerebral hemispheres from birth until puberty. During this period, his argument goes, the dominant hemisphere becomes more and more specialised for language, until, at puberty, all language functions are concentrated in that part of the brain. This process of *interhemispheric specialisation*, and the concomitant loss of *cerebral plasticity*, is held responsible for the alleged fact that after the onset of puberty 'languages have to be taught and learned through a conscious and laboured effort' and that 'foreign accents cannot be overcome easily' (Lenneberg, 1967: 176).

Variations on Lenneberg's hypothesis have been proposed by Seliger (1978), Walsh & Diller (1981) and Scovel (1969, 1988). What these later proposals have in common is that, unlike Lenneberg's, they all allot a special place to the acquisition of accent. Seliger argues that in addition to the process of interhemispheric specialisation there is also one of *intrahemispheric specialisation*, a process of further specification of particular language functions in specific areas of the dominant hemisphere which extends beyond puberty. While this process continues, Seliger claims, brain plasticity remains for those functions not yet localised. This leads him to posit the existence of not one but 'many critical periods, successive and perhaps overlapping, lasting probably throughout one's lifetime, each closing off different acquisition abilities' (Seliger, 1978: 16). Seliger suggests that the ability to master a native accent in a foreign language is lost first and he situates that loss 'not much beyond the onset of puberty in most cases' (p. 16). Walsh & Diller, too, make a distinction between the acquisition of accent and the acquisition of other language skills. They claim, like Seliger, that pronunciation is affected first and that 'foreign accents are difficult to overcome after childhood' (Walsh & Diller, 1981: 18). They base their claim on the argument that pronunciation is a 'lower-order process' which is 'dependent on the early maturing and less adaptive macroneural circuits', while 'higher-order functions', such as grammar, are 'more dependent on the late maturing neural circuits' (Walsh & Diller, 1981:

18). Finally, Scovel posits that there is no critical period for the acquisition of any aspect of language, except pronunciation. Pronunciation is excepted, because 'phonological production is the only aspect of language performance that has a neuromuscular basis'. Learning new words and acquiring morphological and syntactic structures are fundamentally different processes, it is claimed, because, unlike the acquisition of pronunciation, 'none of these require neuromotor involvement; none of them have a "physical reality"' (Scovel, 1988: 101). Scovel assumes that the critical period for the acquisition of accentless speech is closed off at or around age 12. He predicts that those who start to learn a second language after that period will never be able to 'pass themselves off as native speakers phonologically' (p. 185). They will, he claims, 'end up easily identified as non-native speakers of that language' (p. 123).

What is the empirical evidence for the existence of a critical period for the acquisition of a native accent in a foreign language? Let us first consider those studies that have compared eventual phonological attainment by child and adult learners and then turn to a study that was specifically designed to test the hypothesis that a native accent in a foreign language is no longer attainable for adult learners.

Asher & García (1969) asked 71 Cuban immigrants (ages 7–19), most of whom had been in the United States for five years, to read aloud four English sentences. The study also included a control group of 30 native speakers of English. The sentences were tape-recorded and presented to 19 native speaker judges who were asked to rate the sentences on a four-point scale, ranging from 'native' to 'definite foreign accent'. The results indicated that (a) none of the Cuban immigrants had attained a native accent, and that (b) there was a linear relationship between their age on arrival (AA) in the United States and the quality of their pronunciation. Of the subjects with an AA of 1 to 6 years, 68% had a near-native accent and none had a definite foreign accent. Of those with AAs of 7 to 13 years, 41% were judged to have a near-native and 16% a definite foreign accent. Of the oldest arrivals (AA 13 to 19) 66% had a definite foreign accent and only 17% were rated as having a near-native accent.

Seliger, Krashen & Ladefoged (1975) asked 394 immigrants in the United States and Israel whether they thought they would be taken for native speakers of English or Hebrew by native speakers of those languages. The results showed that age of arrival was an important predictor of success in acquiring a native accent. Of those who had arrived before the age of 10, 85% reported their speech to be accentless, whereas only about 7% of those who arrived at age 16 or older reported no accent. Of the studies reviewed in this section, Seliger *et al.*'s is the only one that reports cases of adult learners without a foreign accent. However, it should be emphasised that this was a self-report study: it is by no means certain that native speakers would have judged these learners' speech to be accentless.

Oyama (1976) conducted a study with a group of 60 Italian immigrants in the United States with an AA of 6 to 20 years and a control group of 10 native speakers of English. Subjects were asked to read aloud a short paragraph and to recount a frightening episode in their lives. The paragraphs and the last 45 seconds of each story were played on audiotape to two native speakers of English, who judged the samples for accent on a five-point scale. Oyama (1976: 272) summarises the results of the study as follows: 'The youngest arrivals perform in the range set by the controls, whereas those arriving after about age 12 do not, and substantial accents start appearing much earlier'.

In a study which was primarily concerned with the acquisition of syntax, Patkowski (1980) mentions in passing that he had two native speakers of English rate, on a scale of 0 to 5, the quality of the pronunciation of his subjects, 67 immigrants in the United States from various L1 backgrounds. The data to be judged were passages from oral interviews. Patkowski (1980: 459) found 'strong main effects for age upon arrival'. A re-examination of the data in Patkowski (1990) brought to light that 15 out of 33 subjects who had arrived before the age of 15 obtained ratings of 5, whereas none of those who had arrived after that age were given such a high rating.

Tahta, Wood & Loewenthal (1981) asked their subjects, 109 immigrants in Great Britain from various countries with an AA varying between 6 and 15+ years, to read a short English text. Three native speakers of English judged the recorded passages for degree of accent on a three-point scale, ranging from no foreign accent to 'marked' foreign accent. The results showed that 'age at which L2 acquisition commenced was massively effective' (Tahta *et al.*, 1981: 267). The speech of those starting at age 6 was invariably judged to be accent-free. The percentage of subjects without a foreign accent gradually decreased, and accent scores increased between AA 7 and 12. All of the subjects who had arrived after the age of 12 were judged to have a foreign accent, often a 'marked' one.

In a more recent study, Thompson (1991) collected three different speech samples from 39 Russian-born subjects, who had settled in the United States at different ages, varying between 4 and 42. Two groups of native speakers judged the samples for degree of accent on a five-point scale. The conclusion which Thompson (1991: 195) drew from her study was that age on arrival 'was the best indicator of the accuracy of [the immigrants'] pronunciation in English'. None of the subjects was judged to speak English without a foreign accent, but for subjects with an AA of 10 years or younger only slight foreign accents are reported, with the two subjects in the study with an AA of 4 years receiving the best ratings.

Finally, there are two studies by Flege (Flege, 1988b; Flege & Fletcher, 1992) that ought to be mentioned here. In these studies both learners of English and native speakers of English, who served as controls, were asked to read aloud three short English sentences. These sentences were tape-recorded and presented to native speaker judges, who rated them for degree of foreign accent. The learners in the first study were native speakers of Mandarin and Taiwanese who resided in the United States at the time of the study. One of the groups of learners consisted of speakers of Taiwanese with a mean AA of 7.6 years who had lived in the United States for an average of 12 years. The other groups consisted of speakers of Mandarin and of Taiwanese who had come to the United States as adults. The finding most relevant to the present study was that the learners with an average AA of 7.6 years received much higher ratings for pronunciation than the adult learners, but lower ones than the native speakers of English. One of the experiments reported on by Flege & Fletcher (1992) included a group of Spanish-speaking learners of English who were between 1 and 6 years of age when they arrived in the United States and had received massive exposure to English from age 5 or 6. The age of the subjects varied from 19 to 26 years. In addition, two groups of native speakers of Spanish who had not started to learn English until adulthood participated in the experiment. These two groups differed from each other mainly with respect to length of residence in the United States, which was on average 14.3 years and 0.7 years, respectively. The main finding from this study was that the pronunciation scores assigned to the 'early' learners did not differ significantly from those assigned to the native speakers of English. The scores of the two groups of 'late' learners, on the other hand, were considerably lower. The conclusion which Flege & Fletcher (1992: 385) draw from the combined results of these two studies is that 'a foreign accent first emerges at an age of L2 learning of between 5 and 8 years'.

What conclusions can be drawn from the above comparative studies of phonological attainment in a second language? All the studies present strong evidence that children generally outperform adults in the long run. However, it is not the case that attainment of a native accent is more or less guaranteed, if one starts to learn a second language before puberty. Rather, a learner appears to have a very good chance of attaining a native accent only if s/he starts learning before the age of 6. Between age 6 and puberty the chances of learning to speak another language without a foreign accent appear to become progressively smaller. After puberty, so the results of the studies surveyed suggest, a native accent seems to be no longer attainable. However, it should be pointed out here that these conclusions are based exclusively on studies investigating the acquisition of a second language, English in most cases, by immigrants in predominantly naturalistic settings. None of the studies reviewed here report any training in pronunciation skills. It remains to be seen whether the results from the immigrant studies are generalisable to other learning environments, in which there is much emphasis on phonetic instruction and intensive training in the pronunciation of the target language.

It could be argued that the most critical test of Scovel's version of the Critical Period Hypothesis is provided not by studies of child–adult differences in eventual attainment, but by studies that have been specifically designed to test whether or not it is possible for at least some postpubescent learners to master a native accent in a second language. One of the very few examples of such research is a much-discussed study by Neufeld (1977, 1978, 1979). In a laboratory experiment Neufeld subjected 20 Canadian university students (ages 19–22) to an intensive training in the pronunciation of a number of Chinese and Japanese sound patterns. After receiving 18 hours of instruction the subjects were asked to repeat ten short phrases in each language five times. Their last attempt was recorded on audiotape and the recorded phrases were subsequently played to three native speakers of each language, who were instructed to rate them for accent on a five-point scale. Neufeld reported that nine subjects were judged to be native speakers of Japanese and that eight subjects received native ratings in Chinese. This led him to conclude that adults have not lost the ability to attain a native level of pronunciation in a foreign language. However, as Scovel (1988: 154–9) and Long (1990: 266–8) have pointed out, there are some serious methodological flaws in Neufeld's study, which undermine his conclusions. First of all, the subjects whom Neufeld reported to have been judged native speakers in fact received scores either of 5 ('Unmistakably native with no sign of interference') or of 4 ('Appears native with occasional English-like sounds'). A re-analysis of the scores shows that only one subject got perfect scores in both languages and two more subjects in Japanese only. Secondly, the outcome may have been influenced by the instructions to the judges. They were not told that the speech samples to be judged were produced by English-speaking learners of Japanese and Chinese, but were made to believe that these samples were from Japanese and Chinese immigrants whose pronunciation of the mother tongue might show traces of interference from English. Thirdly, there were no samples from native speakers of Japanese and Chinese serving as controls among the speech data presented to the judges. Finally, the relevance of Neufeld's experiment is further limited by the fact that subjects were not informed about the meaning or the grammatical structure of the phrases they were taught to produce. In fact, it could be argued that Neufeld's study may have demonstrated only that some adults have not lost the ability to imitate unfamiliar sound patterns (see also Neufeld & Schneiderman, 1980). From this we can conclude, therefore, that Neufeld has not proved beyond doubt that adults can learn to speak a second language without a foreign accent.

The present small-scale study is another attempt to test the claim that there is a critical period for accentless speech, using as subjects native speakers of Dutch who had started to learn English on entering secondary education, at or around age 12. Following a suggestion by Long (1990), we included in our study a group of subjects whom experts had designated as exceptionally successful learners of English. Four different speech samples were elicited from the subjects and presented to native speakers of English who rated the samples for accent. The main aim of the study was to establish whether or not there are cases of 'late' learners who have acquired such a good pronunciation of English that they can pass themselves off as native speakers of that language.

Method

Subjects

Three groups of subjects were included in the study: two groups of native speakers of Dutch and one group of native speakers of English.

Group 1 — the control group — consisted of five native speakers of English (three male, two female). They all spoke a variety of English that we regarded as 'neutral' British English in the sense that they did not speak with a noticeable regional accent. Their ages ranged from 21 to 43 years (mean age 30 years). They all had a university background.

Group 2 consisted of ten native speakers of Dutch (eight male, two female) who had been selected for the study because they had been designated by their tutors or colleagues as highly successful learners whose written and spoken English was excellent. The subjects in this group were either reading English at a Dutch university or taught English at a Dutch university or a Dutch college of education. They ranged in age from 23 to 52 years (mean age 37 years). It was expected that, if the study were to yield evidence against the existence of a critical period, this evidence would be provided by subjects in this group.

Group 3 consisted of twelve native speakers of Dutch (five male, seven female) who were either students or lecturers at a Dutch university. These subjects were selected from a larger pool of potential participants on the basis of assessments of the quality of their pronunciation of English, such that the speech of the subjects eventually selected ranged from slightly to fairly heavily accented. It was hoped that this would induce the judges to use the entire range of the rating scale (see below). The subjects in this group were between 19 and 43 years of age (mean age 29 years).

The subjects in Groups 2 and 3 were all late learners, who had started to learn English in the first form of secondary school at or around age 12. At the time of data collection all of them had received between seven and twelve years of instruction in English at Dutch secondary schools and at university. None of them had had contacts with native speakers of English before entering secondary school. None of them had ever visited an English-speaking country before the age of 15.

Elicitation of speech samples

Four different speech samples were collected from the subjects by having them perform four different tasks. They were asked to:

(1) talk in English for about three minutes about their most recent holiday abroad;
(2) read aloud a short English text. This text consisted of 84 words;
(3) read aloud ten short English sentences. The number of words in these sentences varied from five to ten;
(4) read aloud 25 English words. The words were specially chosen so that they included most English phonemes. The length of the words varied from one to five syllables.

These four tasks were included in the study on the assumption that they would allow four different degrees of pronunciation monitoring on the part of the subjects, Task 1 allowing the least degree of monitoring and Task 4 the highest. The idea was that the more subjects would be able to monitor their pronunciation (and would not have to worry about grammar and vocabulary) the better their pronunciation would be and the more it would approximate that of native speakers (see also Dickerson & Dickerson, 1977; Tarone, 1979, 1988; Major, 1987, 1990).

Subjects were tested individually. They performed the four tasks in one session in the sound studio of the Department of Language and Speech of the University of Nijmegen. Their speech was recorded on BASF studio tape. Only one attempt at a recording was made. All subjects had to do the tasks in the same order (1, 2, 3, 4), but the order of the sentences in Task 3 and the order of the words in Task 4 was different for each subject. Subjects were not informed about the aims of the study and were not told beforehand that their speech samples would be rated for degree of accent. When interviewed after task completion, most subjects reported that they did not begin to realise that their pronunciation would be judged until after they had done the second or third task. Subjects were given the opportunity to make a few notes before doing the first task. Between tasks they were allowed to pause briefly and to look over the printed materials before reading them into the microphone. They were instructed to speak or read aloud at their normal rate of speech.

Judges

The speech samples were judged by four native speakers of British English (two male, two female) from York, in the north of England. They were all 'naive' judges with no experience in assessing pronunciation. It was decided to use 'naive' judges because it has been demonstrated in a number of studies (e.g. Scovel, 1981; Flege, 1984) that inexperienced native speakers can reliably judge whether someone speaks with a foreign accent, and because in a recent study (Thompson, 1991), in which both naive and experienced native speakers participated, the former group proved to be less lenient. None of the judges spoke English with a noticeable regional accent. Their ages varied from 19 to 53 years. At the time of the rating experiment one of the judges was a physics teacher at a secondary school and ran an adult education centre, one owned and managed a catering company, one was employed as an occupational therapist and one was a child psychologist working on a research project.

Preparation of speech samples

In order to make sure that the ratings of the speech samples from Task 1 would be based purely on pronunciation and not also on grammar or choice of vocabulary, excerpts of 16 to 20 seconds containing only natural, idiomatic and error-free English were edited from each of the original three-minute samples of spontaneous speech. This was necessary because not all subjects, particularly those in Group 3, were able to talk for the full three minutes without deviating from the native norm with respect to grammar and choice of vocabulary. A 16–20 second passage was thought to be sufficient, because Scovel (1981) has convincingly demonstrated that native speakers can give reliable judgements as to the presence of a foreign accent on the basis of speech samples lasting only eight seconds. For reliable judgments on the basis of even shorter samples see Flege (1984) and Major (1987).

Four different audiotapes were made for each of the four judges. Each tape contained the speech samples supplied by the 27 subjects for *one* of the tasks. The order of the speech samples on each tape was randomised under a number of conditions using an SPSS randomisation programme. Care was taken to ensure that:

- the first two samples on each tape were not from speakers in Group 1 (the native speakers);
- the samples from the native speakers were ordered in such a way that there were never two consecutive samples from this group of subjects within a complete sequence of samples on a given tape;
- the samples from the subjects in Group 2 or 3 were ordered in such a way that there were never more than two consecutive samples from subjects in Group 2 or from subjects in Group 3.

Thus, for each judge there were four audiotapes, one for each task, each tape containing a unique order of speech samples.

A pause of four seconds was inserted after each speech sample, during which the judges could make up their minds. Furthermore, on each tape the samples were preceded by oral instructions to the judges as well as by two practice samples.

Rating procedure

The judges had to rate four tapes, each containing 27 speech samples. The order in which the tapes had to be rated was different for each judge. Prior to rating the samples on a given tape, the judges received both written and oral tape-recorded instructions for their rating task. They were also told that they would be hearing speech samples produced by native speakers of English and by learners of English as a second language, but they were not informed about the proportion of native to non-native speakers. The judges were asked to rate each speech sample for foreign accent on a five-point scale:

(1) Very strong foreign accent: definitely non-native.
(2) Strong foreign accent.
(3) Noticeable foreign accent.
(4) Slight foreign accent.
(5) No foreign accent at all: definitely native.

After the judges had rated the speech samples on one tape, they were given a break before the next tape was presented to them.

Results

The ratings resulting from the four rating tasks have been incorporated in full into Table 1.1, together with the means for groups, tasks, and cells (i.e. group-task combinations). A cursory glance at Table 1.1 immediately reveals the existence of a number of cases that present counter-evidence to Scovel's hypothesis, which, as we have seen, is deterministic in nature and excludes the possibility of subjects from Group 1 being equalled or outperformed by subjects from Groups 2 or 3. The table shows, for example, that subjects 6–11 received perfect scores ('definitely native') on Task 4 and three of them on Task 3 as well, thus equalling or outperforming most native speakers in the study.

In order to get a more global picture of the structure of the ratings, the similarities/dissimilarities between the subjects' score patterns were visualised using the multidimensional scaling programme MINISSA designed by Roskam, Lingoes & Raaijmakers (1986). This procedure represents entities (here: subjects) as points in an n-dimensional space, in such a way that the distances between the points reflect the empirical dissimilarities between the entities as closely as possible. As a measure of the empirical dissimilarities between any two score patterns the 'Euclidian distance' was used, which can be calculated using the routine PROXIMITIES from the SPSSX-programme (1990). A two-dimensional space appeared to be sufficient for the representation of these differences. The resulting MINISSA plot is represented in Figure 1.1.

In this plot numbers 1–5 represent the subjects from Group 1, numbers 6–15 those from Group 2 and numbers 16–27 those from Group 3. As well as plotting the score patterns of the 27 subjects in our study, we also generated and plotted three additional, artificial patterns, which are represented by numbers 28, 29 and 30, to facilitate the interpretation of the MINISSA plot. Number 28 indicates the position a subject would occupy if s/he were given a rating of 1 ('definitely non-native') on all tasks and by all judges. Number 29 would indicate the position of an intermediate subject who scores 3's on all tasks and number 30 would represent someone who is given the 'ideal' score of 5 ('definitely native') for all tasks and by each of the judges. The MINISSA plot shows that the subjects included in Group 2 (the 'excellent' learners of English, numbers 6–15) fall within the same range as the subjects in Group 1 (the native speakers of English, numbers 1–5). The subjects in Group 3 clearly fall outside the range of Groups 1 and 2. It is also remarkable that the four subjects who come closest to the 'ideal' score (number 30 on the plot) are from Group 2 (the 'excellent' learners) and not from the native speaker control group.

Table 1.1 Raw data and mean scores for groups, tasks and cells (= group–task combinations)

Tasks:		1				2				3				4				*Group means:*
Judges:		1	2	3	4	1	2	3	4	1	2	3	4	1	2	3	4	
Group 1	1	3	3	5	5	5	5	5	3	5	3	4	2	5	5	5	5	
	2	3	4	4	4	5	3	3	2	1	3	3	4	5	5	5	4	
	3	4	2	1	4	5	4	4	3	5	3	4	3	5	4	5	5	3.94
	4	5	4	5	4	5	5	5	4	5	3	2	4	5	5	5	5	
	5	2	5	4	3	3	4	3	4	2	3	5	1	5	5	4	4	
Cell means:		3.70				4.00				3.25				4.80				
Group 2	6	3	5	5	5	3	4	4	5	4	5	5	5	5	5	5	5	
	7	5	5	4	5	4	4	3	3	5	4	5	5	5	5	5	5	
	8	4	5	5	5	4	5	5	5	5	5	5	5	5	5	5	5	
	9	3	5	4	5	4	3	3	3	4	5	5	2	5	5	5	5	
	10	4	4	5	5	4	4	3	4	5	5	5	5	5	5	5	5	4.31
	11	3	4	4	4	5	4	5	5	5	5	5	5	5	5	5	5	
	12	3	3	5	5	5	4	5	4	4	3	4	2	5	5	5	4	
	13	4	3	4	5	4	4	3	3	5	5	3	4	5	5	5	5	
	14	4	2	4	4	5	3	3	5	3	1	4	4	5	4	4	4	
	15	2	1	4	5	5	3	4	4	4	4	1	5	4	4	5	5	
Cell means		4.10				4.02				4.28				4.85				
Group 3	16	4	1	3	3	5	2	1	3	5	1	1	1	5	4	4	4	
	17	1	1	1	4	2	2	3	3	1	1	1	5	3	3	4	5	
	18	2	2	4	4	4	3	2	5	3	1	3	1	4	3	4	5	
	19	1	3	1	4	3	3	3	2	1	1	1	1	4	3	4	5	
	20	2	1	1	4	2	2	1	1	1	1	1	1	4	3	4	3	
	21	1	1	1	1	1	2	2	1	1	1	1	1	3	2	4	4	
	22	1	1	1	1	1	1	2	1	1	1	1	1	3	2	3	3	2.35
	23	2	2	4	3	2	3	3	5	1	2	1	1	3	3	4	5	
	24	2	2	3	1	3	4	2	2	1	1	1	1	3	3	4	4	
	25	1	1	1	1	2	2	1	2	1	1	1	1	3	3	4	4	
	26	3	1	4	4	2	3	4	5	1	1	1	1	4	3	5	4	
	27	2	1	1	1	3	3	1	1	5	1	1	3	4	3	4	4	
Cell means:		1.98				2.38				1.40				3.67				
Task means:		3.08				3.29				2.81				4.31				3.37

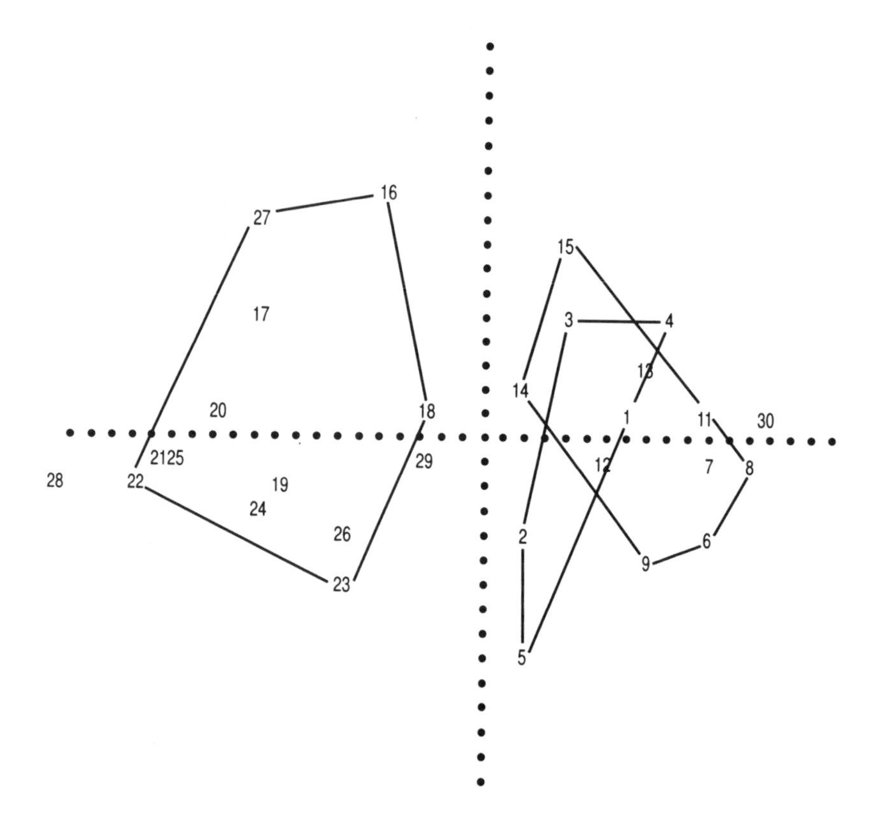

Figure 1.1 MINISSA plot of 30 subjects based on Euclidean distances. Subjects 1–5 = Group1; Subjects 6–15 = Group 2; Subjects 16–27 = Group 3. NB. Numbers 7 & 10 overlap.

The analysis of the ratings was continued with an ANOVA on the raw scores with 'group' as a between-subjects factor and 'task' and 'judge' as within-subjects factors. The absence of a second-order interaction between these three factors, $F(18,216) = 0.56$, $p = 0.554$, allows us to view the relationship between groups and tasks, which, itself, is characterised by a significant interaction, $F(6,72) = 5.90$, $p < 0.001$, as invariant across judges. This result, together with the finding that the inter-judge reliabilities for each task were satisfactory (the values of Cronbach's alpha are 0.85, 0.84, 0.87 and 0.86 for Tasks 1, 2, 3 and 4 respectively), justifies an analysis of the relationship between groups and tasks after averaging scores across judges.

However, in view of the significant interaction between these factors, we have to study the two research questions which are addressed in this paper, relating to group-related and task-related differences in scores respectively, not in terms of main effects but in terms of simple main effects, that is, group differences per task and task differences per group. In order to examine differences between the groups, two contrasts were calculated and tested per task: (i) between Groups 1 and 2 versus Group 3, and (ii) between Group 1 and Group 2. The first contrast was found to be significant: on all tasks the scores for Group 3 were significantly lower than those for Groups 1 and 2 (for the relevant cell means see Table 1.1). The F-values range from 40.17 to 87.18 and are all significant at the 0.001 level. With respect to the second contrast, it can be concluded from Table 1.1 that the group of 'excellent' learners of English was not outperformed by the group of native speakers of English on any of the tasks. In fact, the former group's average score on Task 3, 4.28, was even significantly higher than that obtained by the native speaker group, 3.25, $F(1,24) = 8.63$, $p < 0.01$. The latter group's score on Task 3 drew our attention to a possible counter-example with respect to our expectation that subjects would obtain higher scores as the tasks they had to perform allowed more opportunity for monitoring and that, therefore, the ratings they would be given for the four tasks would exhibit the following order: $4 > 3 > 2 > 1$. As Table 1.1 shows, of the four tasks, Task 3 appears to yield the lowest average score for Group 1. The order of the scores obtained by the other two groups also seems to deviate somewhat from the expected pattern. These findings led us to decide to compare the task differences per group, calculating and testing multiple comparisons using the Tukey procedure. This test revealed that, within all groups, the scores on Task 4 were significantly higher (at the 0.05 level of significance) than those on the other tasks. No statistically significant differences were found for Tasks 1, 2 and 3 within Groups 1 and 2. Therefore, the possible counter-example referred to above does not appear to be statistically significant. However, within Group 3 the scores on Tasks 1 and 2 were significantly higher than those on Task 3, which clearly violates the expected order: the performance of the subjects from Group 3 on this task, which required them to read aloud a number of short English sentences, was unexpectedly poor.

Conclusions and Discussion

The main conclusion that can be drawn from this small-scale study is that there appear to be cases of 'late' second language learners who can pass for native speakers phonologically. The native speaker judges in the study regarded the subjects in Group 1 (the native speakers of English) and those in Group 2 (the highly successful learners of English) as members of the same population. To the judges these two groups were indistinguishable with respect to their pronunciation. This result can be interpreted as providing a challenge to Scovel's claim that there is a biologically constrained period for the acquisition of accent, ending at or around age 12, beyond which it is impossible for learners to acquire such a good pronunciation in a non-native language that they can 'pass themselves off as native speakers' of that language (Scovel, 1988: 185).

It would, of course, be quite premature to claim, on the basis of this result, that there are no biological advantages to an early start in acquiring the pronunciation of a second language. Rather, as a possible explanation for the findings in this study, we would like to suggest that, in some cases at least, the biological disadvantages of a late start may be compensated for by an interaction of certain learner and context variables. The non-native subjects in the present study were all students or lecturers at a Dutch university or teacher training institute. Although all subjects reported that initially their exposure to the English language was largely limited to the two or three hours of instruction a week they received at secondary school, exposure increased dramatically once they were at university. From this time on, they were almost exclusively taught in English, were schooled in phonetics and attended pronunciation tutorials, during which they received intensive training in the pronunciation of the variety of British English known as RP or 'Received Pronunciation'. Studies by Flege & Eefting (1987) and Flege (1990), which focus on the pronunciation of English by native speakers of Dutch, have shown that intensive training in phonetics and pronunciation can be an important determiner of success in the acquisition of accent. In these studies, the subjects who came closest to sounding like a native speaker of English were university students majoring in English who had received special training in phonetics and pronunciation. To use a variant of the title of a paper by Long (1983), this suggests that 'Instruction in the pronunciation of a second language does make a difference', at least for some learners. Furthermore, many subjects in our study, the lecturers in particular, reported intensive contacts with native speakers of English at international conferences and/or during an extended stay in an English-speaking country, usually Great Britain. In addition, all the non-native subjects chose to read English at university and for most of them, particularly the lecturers, it was very important to be able to speak English without a noticeable Dutch accent. In summary, we may conclude that these subjects were highly motivated learners of English, who had furthermore received a great amount of both unstructured and structured target language input during the second phase of the learning process.

In this study we did not carry out a detailed investigation of the specific characteristics of those learners who were highly successful. We do not know, therefore, to what extent these learners differ from less successful learners in terms of cognitive variables such as language aptitude, cognitive style or the use of learning strategies, or in terms of affective variables such as anxiety, empathy or what Guiora (Guiora *et al.*, 1972, 1980; Guiora, 1990, 1991) has referred to as 'ego permeability'. It is obvious that much research will still have to be done in this area: only systematic and detailed studies of the cognitive and affective characteristics of excellent second language learners and of the language input they receive can bring to light which combination(s) of learner characteristics and variables of learning context can compensate for the biological disadvantages of a late start. For a discussion of the role of learner variables see Skehan (1989) and, in particular, Singleton (1989).

In the light of the findings from this study it would seem better to replace the term *critical period*, which excludes the possibility that there are late learners who can learn to speak a second language without a foreign accent, with the term *sensitive period*, which does not exclude this possibility and, at the same time, does not deny that there may be biological advantages to an early start.

In the present study, as in many comparable studies requiring native speakers to rate speech samples on an *n*-point scale, the native speaker judges failed to consistently assign the highest score (5: 'definitely native') to subjects in the native speaker control group. What is more surprising, however, is that four subjects from Group 2 were assigned higher scores than any of the native speakers in the study. A possible explanation for this is suggested by the composition of the native speaker control group (Group 1), the group of highly successful second language learners (Group 2) and the group of judges. The subjects in Group 1 were from the south of England or the Midlands and although they all spoke what we regarded as a 'neutral' variety of British English, there were nevertheless some elements in their pronunciation which may have smacked of a regional accent. The subjects in Group 2 had all been intensively trained to speak the prestigious variety of British English known as RP, which is the variety spoken by, for example, most news-readers and programme-presenters on British national radio and television. The judges were all based in York, in the north of England. It is conceivable that these judges were more inclined to assign the highest score to subjects they regarded as speaking a more neutral variety of English than to those who spoke English with a slight regional accent with which they were not so familiar.

Our expectation that subjects would be assigned higher scores as the tasks they had to perform allowed more monitoring was only partially confirmed. As hypothesised, the subjects obtained the highest scores on Task 4, the wordlist, which enabled them to concentrate fully on their pronunciation. With respect to the other three tasks, our hypothesis was not confirmed. There were no significant differences in the scores assigned to subjects in Groups 1 and 2 on Tasks 1, 2 and 3 and in the scores obtained by subjects in Group 3 on Tasks 1 and 2. On Task 3, which we had expected to yield the highest scores after Task 4, the subjects in Group 3 performed worse than on Tasks 1 and 2. There is not much we can offer in the way of explanation here, but it should be pointed out that all the Dutch subjects in our study were very advanced learners of English. It is conceivable that none of these three tasks posed serious problems to the subjects in terms of vocabulary or grammar, so that they could pay a fair amount of attention to their pronunciation while performing them. For a discussion of a number of other studies which failed to demonstrate hypothesised effects of differences in task on the quality of pronunciation, see Flege (1988a: 373–6).

In this study we have followed Scovel (1988) in assuming that the Critical Period Hypothesis is disconfirmed if 'late' second language learners can be found who have acquired such a good pronunciation of the target language that they can 'pass themselves off as native speakers phonologically' (Scovel, 1988: 185). It is possible, however, that, although a non-native speaker's pronunciation may be judged to be native by native speakers, fine-grained instrumental analyses would bring to light differences between his/her pronunciation and that of a native speaker which are not observable by ear alone. For example, it is an empirical question whether measurements of voice onset time values in the realisation of the English consonants /p/, /t/ and /k/ in prevocalic position, or of the spectral and temporal properties in the realisation of English vowels would show up subtle, but significant differences between native speakers of English and the highly successful learners of English in our study (for examples of such instrumental phonetic research, see Flege & Hillebrand, 1984; Flege & Eefting, 1987; Flege, 1990; Bohn & Flege, 1992). Plans for a follow-up study, in which we intend to subject the speech of the subjects in Group 2 to various instrumental analyses and to relate the results of these analyses to phonetic norms for British English, are in preparation. This type of research can yield interesting information with respect to theories of bilingual speech production. For example, it may shed light on the question whether or not, in the case of exceptionally successful language learners, the phonetic inventories of the first and the second language are stored completely separately in the bilingual brain. However, from the viewpoint of applied linguists and second language learners such research is clearly of less importance. For them it is not very relevant if a second language learner shows differences from native speakers on more and more refined tests, as long as s/he can pass for a native speaker of the target language (Davies, 1991: 166).

Finally, it is important to reiterate that the present study was a small-scale investigation which focused on Dutch learners of a second language which is typologically closely related to their first language, English and Dutch both being Germanic languages. It is conceivable that the results of this study may not be generalisable beyond bilingual speakers of languages belonging to the same language family. One of our main priorities for the future, therefore, is to conduct a study involving highly successful Dutch learners of a language from another language family. This language will probably be French, both for practical and theoretical reasons. French is the most widely taught non-Germanic language in the Netherlands, so it should not be too difficult to find a sufficient number of learners whose spoken French will be designated as excellent by experts in French as a foreign language. More importantly, on a suprasegmental level there are some interesting differences between French and Dutch (or English for that matter). One very striking difference concerns speech rhythm. Whereas in French there is a tendency for each syllable to be allowed an equal period of time (syllable timing), in Dutch and English the accented syllable plays a central role: the duration of an accented syllable plus that of any following unaccented syllables tends to be constant irrespective of the number of unaccented syllables (stress timing) (Gussenhoven & Broeders, 1976). Only by conducting such additional research will it be possible to determine whether the results from the present study are generalisable to other than typologically closely related first and second language pairs.

References

ASHER, J.J. and GARCÍA, R. 1969, The optimal age to learn a foreign language. *The Modern Language Journal* 53, 334–41. Reprinted in KRASHEN, SCARCELLA and LONG (eds) (1982), (pp. 3–12).

BOHN, O.-S. and FLEGE, J.E. 1992, The production of new and similar vowels by adult German learners of English. *Studies in Second Language Acquisition* 14, 131–58.

BROWN, H.D. 1987, *Principles of Language Learning and Teaching* (2nd edn). Englewood Cliffs, NJ: Prentice-Hall.

DAVIES, A. 1991, *The Native Speaker in Applied Linguistics*. Edinburgh: Edinburgh University Press.

DICKERSON, L.J. and DICKERSON, W.B. 1977, Interlanguage phonology: Current research and future directions. In S.P. CORDER and E. ROULET (eds) *The Notions of Simplification, Interlanguages and Pidgins and their Relation to Second Language Pedagogy* (*Actes du 5ème Colloque de Linguistique Appliquée de Neuchâtel*) (pp. 18–29). Genève: Librairie Droz.

FLEGE, J.E. 1984, The detection of French accent by American listeners. *Journal of the Acoustical Society of America* 76, 692–707.

— 1988a, The production and perception of foreign language speech sounds. In H. WINITZ (ed.) *Human Communication and its Disorders. A Review 1988* (pp. 224–401). Norwood, NJ: Ablex Publishing Company.

— 1988b, Factors affecting degree of perceived foreign accent in English sentences. *Journal of the Acoustical Society of America* 84, 70–9.

— 1990, English vowel production by Dutch talkers: More evidence for the 'similar' vs. 'new' distinction. In J. LEATHER and A.R. JAMES (eds) *New Sounds* 90 (pp. 255–93). Amsterdam: University of Amsterdam.

FLEGE, J.E. and EEFTING, W. 1987, Cross-language switching in stop consonant perception and production by Dutch speakers of English. *Speech Communication* 6, 185–202.

FLEGE, J.E. and FLETCHER, K.L. 1992, Talker and listener effects on degree of perceived foreign accent. *Journal of the Acoustical Society of America* 91, 370–89.

FLEGE, J.E. and HILLEBRAND, J. 1984, Limits in phonetic accuracy in foreign language speech production. *Journal of the Acoustical Society of America* 76, 708–21.

GUIORA, A.Z. 1990, A psychological theory of second language production. *Toegepaste Taalwetenschap in Artikelen* 37 (2), 15–23.

— 1991, The two faces of language ego. *Toegepaste Taalwetenschap in Artikelen* 41 (3), 5–14.

GUIORA, A.Z., ACTON, W.R., ERARD, R. and STRICKLAND, F.W. 1980, The effects of benzodiazepine (valium) on permeability of language ego boundaries. *Language Learning* 30, 351–63.

GUIORA, A.Z., BEIT-HALLAHMI, B., BRANNON, R.C.L., DULL, C.Y. and SCOVEL, T.S. 1972, The effects of experimentally induced changes in ego states on pronunciation ability in a second language: An exploratory study. *Comprehensive Psychiatry* 13, 421–8.

GUSSENHOVEN, C. and BROEDERS, T. 1976, *The Pronunciation of English*. Groningen: Wolters-Noordhoff-Longman.

KRASHEN, S.D., SCARCELLA, R.S. and LONG, M.H. (eds) 1982, *Child–Adult Differences in Second Language Acquisition*. Rowley, MA: Newbury House.

LENNEBERG, E.H. 1967, *Biological Foundations of Language*. New York: Wiley.

LONG, M.H. 1983, Does second language instruction make a difference? A review of research. *TESOL Quarterly* 17, 359–82.

— 1990, Maturational constraints on language development. *Studies in Second Language Acquisition* 12, 251–85.

MAJOR, R.C. 1987, A model of interlanguage phonology. In G.L. IOUP and S.H. WEINBERGER (eds) *Interlanguage Phonology: The Acquisition of a Second Language Sound System* (pp. 101–24). New York: Newbury House.

— 1990, L2 acquisition, L1 loss, and the critical period hypothesis. In J. LEATHER and A.R. JAMES (eds) *New Sounds 90* (pp. 14–25). Amsterdam: University of Amsterdam.
NEUFELD, G.G. 1977, Language learning ability in adults: A study on the acquisition of prosodic and articulatory features. *Working Papers on Bilingualism* 12, 46–60.
— 1978, On the acquisition of prosodic and articulatory features in adult language learning. *The Canadian Modern Language Review* 34, 163–74.
— 1979, Towards a theory of language learning ability. *Language Learning* 29, 227–41.
NEUFELD, G.G. and SCHNEIDERMAN, E. 1980, Prosodic and articulatory features in adult language learning. In R.C. SCARCELLA and S.D. KRASHEN (eds) *Research in Second Language Acquisition* (pp. 105–9). Rowley, MA: Newbury House.
OYAMA, S. 1976, A sensitive period for the acquisition of a nonnative phonological system. *Journal of Psycholinguistic Research* 5, 261–83. Reprinted in KRASHEN, SCARCELLA and LONG (eds) (1982) (pp. 20–38).
PATKOWSKI, M.S. 1980, The sensitive period for the acquisition of syntax in a second language. *Language Learning* 30, 449–72. Reprinted in KRASHEN, SCARCELLA and LONG (eds) (1982) (pp. 52–63).
— 1990, Age and accent in a second language: A reply to James Emil Flege. *Applied Linguistics* 11, 73–89.
PENFIELD, W. 1963, *The Second Career*. Boston: Little, Brown.
ROSKAM, E., LINGOES, J. and RAAIJMAKERS, M. 1986, *Kunst Program MINISSA*. Nijmegen: University of Nijmegen.
SCOVEL, T. 1969, Foreign accents, language acquisition, and cerebral dominance. *Language Learning* 19, 245–54.
— 1981, The recognition of foreign accents in English and its implications for psycholinguistic theories of language acquisition. In J.-G. SAVARD and L. LAFORGE (eds) *Proceedings of the 5th Congress of L'Association Internationale de Linguistique Appliquée* (pp. 389–401). Québec: Les Presses de L'Université Laval.
— 1988, *A Time to Speak. A Psycholinguistic Inquiry into the Critical Period for Human Speech*. Rowley, MA: Newbury House.
SELIGER, H.W. 1978, Implications of a multiple critical periods hypothesis for second language learning. In W.C. RITCHIE (ed.) *Second Language Acquisition Research. Issues and Implications* (pp. 11–19). New York: Academic Press.
SELIGER, H.W., KRASHEN, S.D. and LADEFOGED, P. 1975, Maturational constraints in the acquisition of second language accent. *Language Sciences* 36, 20–2. Reprinted in KRASHEN, SCARCELLA and LONG (eds) (1982) (pp. 13–19).
SINGLETON, D. 1989, *Language Acquisition: The Age Factor*. Clevedon: Multilingual Matters.
SKEHAN, P. 1989, *Individual Differences in Second-Language Learning*. London: Edward Arnold.
SPSSX Reference Guide 1990. Chicago, IL: SPSSX Incorporated.
TAHTA, S., WOOD, M. and LOEWENTHAL, K. 1981, Foreign accents: Factors relating to transfer of accent from the first language to a second language. *Language and Speech* 24, 265–72.
TARONE, E. 1979, Interlanguage as chameleon. *Language Learning* 29, 181–91.
— 1988, *Variation in Interlanguage*. London: Edward Arnold.

THOMPSON, I. 1991, Foreign accents revisited: The English pronunciation of Russian immigrants. *Language Learning* 41, 177–204.
WALSH, T.M. and DILLER, K. C. 1981, Neurolinguistic considerations on the optimum age for second language learning. In K.C. DILLER (ed.) *Individual Differences and Universals in Language Learning Aptitude* (pp. 3–21). Rowley, MA: Newbury House.

2 Multi-Competence and Effects of Age

VIVIAN COOK

Introduction

The term *'multi-competence'* was introduced to describe 'the compound state of a mind with two grammars', contrasted with *'mono-competence'*, the state of the mind with only one (Cook, 1991). While the underlying concept has often been taken for granted in bilingualism research, it is by no means widely accepted in second language acquisition research, which tends, as we shall see, to treat second language (L2) competence as if the L2 is in a different mind from the first. A series of papers has looked at the use of multi-competence in different contexts (Cook, 1992, 1994). The present paper relates multi-competence to the issue of age, mostly within the Universal Grammar (UG) theory of second language acquisition. This means first of all establishing the nature of a multi-competence second language acquisition programme, then seeing how it might accommodate age.

The effects of age on L2 learning are far from as clear-cut as popular wisdom, or indeed some linguists, would have us believe. In their respective reviews of age, Krashen, Long & Scarcella (1979), Cook (1986), and Singleton (1989) come to general, if tentative, solutions, expressed by Singleton (1989: 266) as follows:

> The one interpretation of the evidence which does not appear to run into contradictory data is that in naturalistic situations those whose exposure to an L2 begins in childhood in general eventually surpass those whose exposure begins in adulthood, even though the latter usually show some initial advantage over the former.

Cook (1986) concentrated on the methodological limitations of the research literature, looking particularly askance at the over-reliance on educated immigrants as subjects, on English as the L2, on Indo-European languages as the first language (L1), on the USA as the main country of immigration, on the limited aspects of language tested in the research, and on the learners' date of arrival rather than on their age of start. Within the overall framework of second language acquisition research the benefits and disadvantages of age still seem far from established. Certainly it is hard to find an overall critical period effect with a particular cut-off age. In addition it should not be forgotten that age is a factor from birth to death. The relationship of age to second language acquisition is not just the difference between children and adults but might also involve second language acquisition in old age (see, for instance, Clyne, 1977).

Multi-Competence and 'Failure'

Any cursory reading of the first language acquisition literature comes up with a picture of excitement and wonder at the child's amazing ability to acquire language. A similar reading of the L2 literature soon produces the opposite impression; most researchers seem perplexed and concerned by how bad people are at learning L2s. All children magically acquire their L1 to a high level of knowledge after a few years. Many L2 learners achieve only a minimal L2 competence after long years of struggle and effort. A main goal for second language acquisition research is seen as explaining this dismal failure. One historical basis for the concept of interlanguage was Selinker's observation that 95% of L2 learners fail to achieve 'absolute success in a second language' (Selinker, 1972: reprint, 33f.). The general negative view can be exemplified more recently in Bley-Vroman (1989: 43), for instance, who discusses 'nine fundamental characteristics of adult foreign language learning' of which 'few are controversial'; the first two are 'lack of success' and 'general failure'. This 'failure' is used by Schachter (1988) and Bley-Vroman (1989) in particular to argue that second language acquisition differs from first language acquisition in being cut off from UG and has to find a substitute channel for acquiring language. One argument is that knowledge of the L2 is not so complete or so good as knowledge of the L1; Schachter (1988: 224) claims 'Most proficient ESL speakers do not have fully formed determiner systems, aspectual systems, or tag question systems'. L2 learners rarely attain the same level of knowledge in their L2 as in their L1. This is taken to indicate lack of access to UG. Furthermore, L2 learners regularly get 'fossilised' at some stage rather than progressing inevitably to full native competence. Schachter's example is the over-use of the present indicative tense by English learners of Spanish. As no L1 children get stuck in this way, UG is not available for learning the L2.

This no-access argument has been related to the learner's age in experiments by Johnson & Newport (1991). Their main testing area is the subjacency relation seen in ungrammatical sentences such as:

*What did Sally watch how Mrs Gomez makes?

versus grammatical sentences such as:

What did the teacher know that Janet liked?

Subjacency is a highly technical area of principles and parameters theory that was fashionable during the 1980s but became largely subsumed under other areas such as the Empty Category Principle (Cook & Newson, forthcoming) as the theory developed. Syntactic movement in human languages is limited by the constraint that the element that is being moved must not cross more than one of certain types of boundaries called 'bounding nodes'. Sentences like:

*What did Sally watch how Mrs Gomez makes?

are ruled out because *what* crosses more than one bounding node. Johnson & Newport tested Chinese learners of English who would not have needed subjacency for syntactic movement in Chinese. The results showed that the ability to detect the ungrammaticality of such sentences varies straightforwardly with age: the younger the learners had arrived in the US the better they were at subjacency, ranging from those who had arrived aged 4–7 up to those who had arrived as adults (i.e. not age of start but age of arrival, when they might or might not have encountered English previously). One of the causes of L2 failure, even within the UG model, seems to be the age of the learner.

What is the source of this aura of failure that envelopes second language acquisition research? A person learning to skate does not normally consider themselves a failure for not competing in the Olympic Games; the child who is learning physics at school is not considered a failure for not mastering quantum theory; a child learning an L1 is not thought of as a defective adult native speaker but as a child in his or her own right. In all these other cases the learner's progress is not measured against an external target of perfection but set against standards appropriate to the learner's own nature. Yet second language acquisition research has somehow accepted that the valid target for the L2 learner is the monolingual. Most research compares L2 learners implicitly with L1 speakers; the typical research methodology uses grammaticality judgments, obligatory contexts, or elicited imitation, all defined by native usage. The target the learners are supposedly aiming at, even if few of them achieve, is the competence of the monolingual, not the competence peculiar to L2 speakers. Failure is defined with reference to monolingual native speakers — the one thing that L2 learners can never be by definition. The goal of second language acquisition is Selinker's successful 5% — the 'balanced' bilingual or 'ambilingual', as Halliday, McIntosh & Strevens (1964) neatly call it. Yet such ambilinguals form a small minority of those who have learnt an L2. Taking them as the paradigm example automatically leads to negative conclusions about L2 learning. Measured against the yardstick of 100% monolingual competence, the L2 knowledge of a learner ranges from 0% to 100%. As learners seldom approach the upper limit, L2 learning has been seen in terms of lack of success; few bilinguals succeed in achieving or maintaining an equal balance between L1 and L2 knowledge.

But suppose the L2 learner is acquiring something extra rather than a pale imitation of the L1 — the vocabulary, syntax, and so on, of the L1 *plus* the vocabulary, syntax, and so on, of the L2. The knowledge of the L2 increases the L2 user's capabilities beyond those of a monolingual, rather than being confining them to defective L1 knowledge. Measured against the 100% of a person who knows one language, the balanced bilingual is functioning at 200%; L2 learners of lesser achievement are functioning at levels between 100% and 200%. Those who start from the balanced bilingual see the L2 learner as a failure for not achieving full L2 competence; even bilinguals, according to Grosjean (1989: 5), 'often assume and amplify the monolingual view and hence criticize their own language competence'. Those who start from the bilingual view see the learners as a success in their own right in going beyond the initial L1, to whatever degree.

In many ways the second language acquisition literature could be considered discriminatory. We (and I include myself in these strictures as much as anybody) have been looking down at the pitiful attempts of the L2 user to attain the lofty heights of the monolingual. Perhaps L2 users should have been looking down from *their* lofty heights at the impoverished lives of monolinguals straitjacketed by one language, one culture, one way of thinking. Whatever the L2 user has achieved exceeds the capabilities of monolinguals, rather than falling short. The pejorative terminology applied to L2 learners resembles a power play by natives who want to keep control of their language, and so deny the rights of non-natives, parallel to the attempts to maintain the position of English across the world at the expense of the Third World (Phillipson, 1992). In other research areas linguists have learnt to speak in terms of differences between people rather than deficits — race, sex, class, and so on; we should try to recognise the difference of the L2 user as a unique human being rather than as a defective monolingual, just as blacks are not defective whites, women are not defective men, and academics are not defective navvies.

The discussion of age in L2 learning is indeed dominated by failure or success in native terms. One example is the question of accent. Asher & García (1969) had native speakers judge 'accent'; Seliger *et al.* (1975) asked learners to report how long they took to lose their 'foreign accent'; Oyama (1976) measured assessment of learners' foreign accent by linguistic students. One might point to the looseness and subjectiveness of the concept of accent as compared, say, to a proper phoneme and allophone inventory of the learner's speech. But what could betray more blatantly that monolingual standards are being applied than using native accent as the yardstick? Why are L2 users considered deficient if they do not *sound* like natives? Are women condemned for not sounding like men? Why should the ability to have this nebulous accent be so crucial? For example, a test of the teachability of pronunciation showed that 18 hours of pronunciation teaching could make 9 out of 20 Canadians indistinguishable from native speakers of Japanese (Neufeld, 1978). What's the point? They are not Japanese and will never for a moment be able to pass for Japanese; they should sound like effective bilinguals.

The early work on interlanguage drew on the 1960s independent grammars assumption (Cook, 1993) — the belief that the child should be treated as a speaker of a language of its own rather than as a defective speaker of adult language who has inefficiently mastered the rules, perhaps first articulated in McNeill (1966). Taking this seriously means discovering the learner's own grammar, not measuring how successfully he or she approximates the monolingual grammar, thus avoiding what Bley-Vroman (1983) calls the Comparative Fallacy. Methodologically the criteria in the age research always seem to be derived from native grammars. Johnson & Newport (1991) for instance asked whether L2 learners come up to scratch compared to native speakers. Tut tut they don't. But might the learners have an alternative grammar rather than a defective grammar? Research based on the monolingual grammar is confined to making conclusions about similarities and differences; it can never reveal a system that is totally different from the native and show the true nature of multi-competent knowledge unfiltered by the native grammar.

The foundation of second language acquisition research has to be multi-competence — the complex supersystem of language knowledge possessed by those who use more than one language. The effects of age should be ascertained by looking at the language of L2 learners in their own right, not by seeing how they fall short of natives. However much the interlanguage researchers protested that they treated the learner's system as independent, their very research techniques sooner or later involved the native target. The question about the relationship of age to second language acquisition should not then be couched in terms of failure; young learners may or may not acquire different knowledge of the L2 than older learners; this is an empirical fact that current research has still not established properly. What is crucial is to discover their own grammars, however different these may be from natives'.

Age and Multi-Competence

An entry point to the discussion of age and multi-competence is the development of growth and non-growth models of UG. The growth version of UG associated with Borer & Wexler (1987) claims that the principles and parameters of UG do not all necessarily come into being at the same time; a biologically predetermined programme allows them to appear gradually in the child's mind. The non-growth version suggests that all the principles and parameters are present from the outset; they cannot be seen in the child's speech because of the various processing systems for language the child has not yet evolved, say the short-term memory capacity necessary to produce longer sentences. In terms of L1 acquisition the choice between these alternatives is impossibly hard to decide; how can you tell an invisible principle that is present in the child's mind but never used because of the other restrictions on the child from a principle that is altogether absent from the child's mind, if you do not have a full psychological account of the development of language processing, since in both cases something will be missing from the child's speech?

A further problem is what is meant by age. Chronological age is a meaningless variable in itself; like time, we can only perceive it in terms of change: no change, no age. Hence age might mean change in the physiology of the brain areas, muscles, or auditory equipment involved in speech; older learners may be physically different from younger learners. Or age might mean mental change — where the person is on the Piagetan sequence of cognitive development, how their short-term memory capacity or structures have developed, and so on. Or age might be social development — the forms of interaction typical at particular ages. All of these have indeed been put forward to explain the alleged effects of age and the age changes are in some way verifiable independently of the L2 evidence. But none of them is directly relevant to the UG model of acquisition, since this does not take account of language development, only of the logical problem of language acquisition, and does not see the language faculty as depending in any way on other mental faculties. Blaming one or other of these for age effects is talking in terms of another model.

We need then to look for other solutions. Why do the grammars of L2 users apparently vary according to the age at which they started L2 learning, judging from Johnson & Newport's work with subjacency? One possibility is indeed that UG is not available to the older L2 learners. But much of the L2 research, such as Bley-Vroman *et al.* (1988), shows that UG is not completely unavailable; scores are always better than chance even if consistently below natives'. Older L2 learners have poor access to UG rather than no access. Another possible solution is a variation on the growth model. Children acquire the L1 in sequence; perhaps subjacency has to come at a particular time in the sequence to be usable, like Konrad Lorenz imprinting his ducks within the critical period. L2 learners of different ages are at different points in this developmental unfolding of principles and parameters. Getting subjacency in the L2 out of step with the maturational sequence may be a handicap and stop it being used as efficiently.

The other possibility is, however, to invoke the nature of multi-competence. Why should multi-competent speakers of two languages have the same grammar of *either* language? My own research has suggested that multi-competence should be treated as a single system; the L1 and L2 systems are symbiotic within the same mind, as is clearly evident, for example, in the complex phenomenon of code-switching. The effects of a UG principle are not therefore necessarily the same for this compound multi-competent state as for a monolingual state. Again the L2 user's grammar must be treated as having its own nature, not as deviant from the monolingual. Some aspects of UG might indeed only become apparent in people who know more than one language. The question is then: do L2 learners who start at different ages acquire different multi-competences?

Age and Simultaneous Acquisition

One of the questions that immediately arises with multi-competence is whether the two languages form one overall system in the mind (wholistic multi-competence) or two (separatist multi-competence). This is a derivative question the answer to which does not affect the notion of multi-competence itself since, at some level, the two languages form part of the same mind by definition, otherwise we would be dealing with people with two heads. Cook (1992) reviewed evidence that minds with two languages are in general different from those with only one — that multi-competence is a different state of mind from monolingualism — concluding that this is true to some extent of L1 and L2 knowledge, metalinguistic awareness, and cognitive processing.

In several areas of psychology the problem of whether the L2 user has two systems or one might well be considered a non-question. Anderson (1983) for example considers 'the adult human mind is a unitary construction'. He refuses to distinguish language from other cognitive systems and, by extension, the L1 from the L2; they are all part of the same network. Indeed he often uses classroom L2 learning as an example of his all-purpose theory of learning. This is discussed further in Cook (1993). Other network theories such as connectionism appear equally committed to the mind as a single organism, with L2 learning being a matter of increasing the strength of certain connections (Gasser, 1990; Sokolik & Smith, 1992). More crucially for our current concerns, it appears to be a standard axiom in bilingualism research that bilinguals are not two monolinguals in the same head: 'it is clear that a reasonable account of bilingualism cannot be based on a theory which assumes monolingual competence as its frame of reference' (Romaine, 1989). The overall emphasis in bilingualism studies is on acceptance of the L2 user *as an L2 user* to be measured by the standards of L2 users, not by those of monolinguals. The L2 user is not an imitation monolingual in the L2 but a genuine bilingual. The 'ultimate attainment' of an L2 is not, and could never be, monolingual competence.

It is mainly then within second language acquisition research that the concept of multi-competence needs to be asserted. As Sridhar & Sridhar (1986: 13) point out, 'Paradoxical as it may seem, second language acquisition researchers seem to have neglected the fact that the goal of SLA is bilingualism'. The question is at what level or in what areas the mind separates the two languages into separate systems. It might be that the core UG areas are inseparable in the two languages, hence the powerful influence of L1 parameter settings on the knowledge of the L2, or it might be that UG cannot be used for an L2 and so the two systems are organised in utterly different ways, as those who support alternatives to UG in L2 learning suggest. It might be that there is a single lexicon for both languages in which each word is branded with its language. Cook (1992) examined the evidence for wholistic versus separatist multi-competence in the areas of the lexicon, code-switching, language processing, physical storage of language in the brain, and the relationship between L1 and L2 proficiency, but not syntax, concluding that 'the two systems are more closely linked than had been previously suspected'.

But these types of evidence are largely concerned with adults who have reached their final state of L2 learning. The division between separatist and wholistic multi-competence may however depend on age, defined in terms both of the mental state at the time at which the people were tested and at the time at which the L2 acquisition started. Let us take the extreme test-case of the simultaneous acquisition of two languages in young children. Again, as with bilingualism, one should not perhaps be too pernickety about defining simultaneous acquisition. The most extreme form is perhaps de Houwer (1990: 71) for instance who records the languages used to her subject in the maternity ward ('English spoken to her by her mother, and Dutch by her father and various members of the nursing staff'). Like the usual arguments against the idealisation to linguistic competence, there could be an argument that the balanced bilingual and the child identically exposed to two languages are fictions that obscure the normal situation. If second language acquisition is restricted to those who achieve balanced bilingualism, it excludes all but a minute proportion of L2 learners; if we restrict simultaneous acquisition to those children who have equal amounts of both languages from maternity ward onwards, these would be so rare as to be virtually non-existent. This does not mean of course that such cases are not interesting as the 'purest' evidence and hence the easiest to research.

The questions that researchers have usually asked about simultaneous bilingualism are whether the child's two languages develop separately — sometimes called the Independent Development Hypothesis — and whether bilingual acquisition follows the same path as monolingual acquisition. The evidence that is cited is extremely mixed and goes back many years, usually at least to Ronjat (1913) and Leopold (1939–49); reviews can be found in McLaughlin (1984) and de Houwer (1990). McLaughlin's review reports, mostly in terms of language processing and memory, that 'research with bilingual children does not support the notion of a dual language system' (McLaughlin, 1984: 195). On the other hand, de Houwer (1990) finds largely the same literature much more ambivalent when restricted to genuinely simultaneous acquisition;

> there is as little positive evidence for the position that bilingual children develop two separate linguistic systems from the earliest stages of acquisition on as there is for the claim that bilingual children start out with a single linguistic system which is later differentiated or separated into two linguistic systems. (de Houwer, 1990: 49)

Let us then review briefly the evidence in some of the relevant areas of research with young bilingual children. While there are many general studies, those directed at any specific area of language seem small in number and far from satisfactory.

Vocabulary

The question that has been most researched is whether children mix the vocabularies of the two languages in the same sentence. Ronjat (1913) originally claimed there was no lexical confusion between languages. Burling (1959), however, reported a boy who first used Garo sentence structure with English words, later the reverse. Leopold (1939: 179) found that 'Words from the two languages did not belong to two speech systems but to one...'. Taeschner (1983) studied two children learning Italian and German; she found an initial stage at which the children had one lexical system, which separated at the next stage into two lexicons with one syntax. Tabouret-Keller (1962) found mixed early sentences with unequal proportions from the vocabulary of the two languages. Swain & Wesche (1975) described lexical mixing between French and English with examples such as *Quelle couleur your poupée*?; de Houwer (1990) observed a Dutch child learning English and Dutch and found only 4.3% mixed sentences addressed to Dutch speakers, 3.9% to English, and 2.5% and 0.9% that were balanced between the two languages ('Dutlish', as she calls it). While attacking Taeschner's methodology and analysis, de Houwer herself does not use vocabulary in her conclusions other than to point to the non-existence of an early stage at which the children have a single lexicon for both languages.

Much of this research is notionally about vocabulary in that it simply categorises the words that occur in the children's speech into L1 or L2. This provides little information on what the child means by the words it uses — are meanings constant across languages, is a word misused in one language because of its meaning in another language, and so on? The research does not use linguistic ideas of vocabulary or modern ideas of vocabulary acquisition, say the acquisition of argument structure; it uses words as isolated atoms of language which either occur or don't occur. It is not a question of two vocabulary systems so much as two word-lists. This commonly found separation between the two lexicons contrasts with the extensive research with adults that shows a single shared lexicon, for example Beauvillain & Grainger (1987). It might be that the two concepts of vocabulary and the two approaches to research are incommensurable, or it might be that there is a genuine difference between children who keep the lexicons separate and adults who have integrated the two lexicons into one. Without more specific research there is little to show whether the two lexicons, as opposed to the two word-lists, form one system or two.

Pronunciation

Most of the bilingualism research simply ignores pronunciation, for example de Houwer (1990). Much of the relevant research furthermore does not use systematic ideas of phonology. Leopold (1947) reports some confusion between the sounds of the two languages and some carryover of phonological processes from one language to the other, as does Ruke-Dravina (1967); Fantini (1985) and Burling (1959) describe children in whom the phonology of one language takes over. Oksaar (1970), however, studied a child who kept the pronunciation of the two languages separate. Essentially these case studies represent every possibility from totally merged systems to totally separate. At best they can provide counter-instances to any absolute claim that *all* bilingual children necessarily have merged or separate pronunciation systems. Much phonetic work has indeed shown that adult bilinguals effectively have a single phonological system for Voice Onset Time (see, for example, Nathan, 1987).

Syntax

Syntax is usually handled in the earlier literature of simultaneous bilingualism as an offshoot of the study of vocabulary and pronunciation rather than in its own right. The question as always is: does the child keep the two systems separate? Ronjat (1913) found few signs of syntactic interference between the two languages. The initial stage of the child's word order in Leopold (1939) appeared to belong to neither language but to express semantic meaning. The sentences produced by the child in Burling (1959) belonged clearly to one language or the other, even when the vocabulary was mixed. Morphological borrowing from English to Estonian occurred in Vihman (1982). Swain & Wesche (1975) found some French structures occurring in English, for example *They open, the windows?* Volterra & Taeschner (1978) however described a stage when children had two lexicons but a single syntactic system that was neither German nor Italian; the child expressed possession in both languages as Noun + Noun *Giulia Buch* (Julia's book) or *Giulia giamma* (Julia's pyjamas).

De Houwer (1990) concentrated on the question of whether the two syntactic systems are separate, finding that the languages (Dutch and English) are kept distinct in gender; bound morphemes such as plural stay in one language; the child mostly uses OV word order in Dutch and VO in English. At all stages the child keeps the languages separate. However, apart from word order, as she points out, Dutch and English are fairly similar in syntax. She also finds 'It is quite striking that the many changes in Kate's two language systems take place at the same time' (de Houwer, 1990: 39).

The DUFDE group directed by Jürgen Meisel — reported, for example, in Meisel (1990a) — have looked at young children learning French and German simultaneously. Meisel (1990b) finds the evidence provided by

Volterra & Taeschner (1978) unconvincing as a demonstration of a clear stage of a single syntactic system; the children had distinct word orders in the two languages, similar but not identical to monolingual children. His conclusion is that 'fusion is not necessarily a characteristic of bilingual language development, but mixing may occur until code-switching is firmly established as a strategy of bilingual pragmatic competence'.

To sum up, the consensus seems to be that, after an initial semantically organised phase, children keep the systems of the two languages distinct, essentially the model presented in Volterra & Taeschner (1978) or Swain & Wesche (1975), except in so far as 'code-switching and mixing are a normal part of bilingual behaviour, both of the child's and the parents'' (Genesee, 1989). The greatest contrast is with the research into adult bilingualism where mostly at the vocabulary level, and sometimes at the phonological level, a single system seems to be involved. But, as we have seen, the evidence is in fact shaky; a consistent account treating language rigorously in terms of vocabulary, pronunciation, and syntax does not exist.

So what for multi-competence? At first sight the implication is that lack of mixing shows two systems; mixing shows one. But keeping two languages separate does not mean that they do not form part of the same system. The system I use for hand-writing is quite different from the one I use for word-processing; there is no way in which I mix them; yet no one would claim that I speak two languages simply because I have two different ways of realising written English. The polylectalists pointed out that all speakers switch continuously from one system to another, else they would not be able to understand children or old age pensioners, Bristol shop assistants or High Court judges. 'Competence is polylectal' (Bailey, 1973). Any language use involves switching from one style or register to another. We do not therefore claim that monolingual speakers have many language systems in their minds and marvel how they keep them separate; instead we believe they have a single language system. Lack of mixing in children no more shows that two systems are involved than does the fact I consistently speak to my cat differently than to the university vice-chancellor. The research into simultaneous acquisition has usually answered the question whether children differentiate two languages, not the question whether the languages form one system. Genesee claims, for example, 'To uphold the unitary system hypothesis one would need to establish that, all things being equal, bilingual children use items from both languages indiscriminately in all contexts' (Genesee, 1989: 165); this same criterion would prove that monolinguals speak many languages. Arbitrary mixing would indeed show no system at all rather than one system, which might well distinguish different forms or vocabulary for different uses, as it does in monolinguals.

Let us put this within the context of current UG theory. The Lexical Parameterisation Hypothesis claims that parameters are part of the lexicon; we do not know the values for the governing category principle in Binding Theory for English, Japanese or Icelandic; we know the setting of the lexical items *himself, zibun,* or *hann* (Wexler & Manzini, 1987). The Functional Parameterisation Hypothesis extends this by claiming that parameters are attached to the lexical entries for functional categories (Ouhalla, 1991). To take the example of the Agreement Phrase, the English AGRP has set the opacity parameter to opaque and so forbids Verb movement, while the French AGRP has set the value to transparent and so allows Verb movement; hence the normality of *Jean embrasse souvent Marie* (John kisses often Marie) and the abnormality of **John kisses often Marie*; the English verb *kiss* cannot cross over the boundary of the English AGRP (Pollock, 1989).

Both of these hypotheses take the view that syntax is invariant; languages differ in their lexicons: 'language acquisition is in essence a matter of determining lexical idiosyncrasies' (Chomsky, 1989: 44). Lexical parameterisation takes the view that the lexicon consists of lexical entries for substantive items such as nouns, verbs, reflexive anaphors, etc., giving their meaning, phonological form and syntactic properties. Children learn these essentially one at a time; when they learn *himself* they acquire its setting for the governing category parameter. The functional parameterisation view envisages an extended lexicon which includes entries for more abstract functional categories such as the Complement Phrase and Agreement Phrase with parameter settings. When children acquire a functional phrase, they start acquiring the parameter settings that go with it.

Lexical parameterisation then fits neatly with the picture of early bilingualism we have been reporting. Children separate the substantive vocabularies because each lexical entry is separate: English *man* and French *homme* are two items in one extended vocabulary, as they are for adult bilinguals. As such the entries project their own syntactic properties on sentences in which the words occur. It is no more surprising that children fail to mix vocabularies than that English adults fail to mix the words cat and chewing gum. There is one multi-competence lexicon with separate entries for each item.

Functional parameterisation raises a further range of issues that require specific research to tackle. There might be separate entries for functional categories in each language, each with a parameter value assigned to it. In this case there is a single overall knowledge of language relying on principles and parameters with language separation maintained as different lexical entries. There might be only one entry possible for each functional category with a parameter attached that has two strengths, switching from one to the other according to which language is involved. The choice between these alternative can be tested through code-switching. In the one case the choice is either/or; a functional phrase in code-switching should keep to one language in terms of its parametric values. This could be interpreted as an extension of the government model of code-switching proposed by Di Sciullo *et al.* (1986) in which governed elements stay in the same language as their governor or as a variant on the Matrix Language Frame Model of Myers-Scotton (1992) in which one language acts as the dominant matrix. In the other case the choice is more/less. Functional phrases mix elements within the phrase with a less clear demarcation.

References

ANDERSON, J.R. 1983, *The Architecture of Cognition*. Cambridge, MA: Harvard University Press.

ASHER, J. and GARCÍA, R. 1969, The optimal age to learn a foreign language. *Modern Language Journal* 38, 334–41.

BAILEY, C-Y. 1973, *Variation and Linguistic Theory*. Arlington, VA: Center for Applied Linguistics.

BEAUVILLAIN, C. and GRAINGER, J. 1987, Accessing interlexical homographs: Some limitations of a language-selective access. *Journal of Memory and Language* 26, 658–72.

BLEY-VROMAN, R.W. 1983, The comparative fallacy in interlanguage studies: The case of systematicity. *Language Learning* 33, 1–17.

— 1989, The logical problem of second language learning. In S. GASS and J. SCHACHTER (eds) *Linguistic Perspectives on Second Language Acquisition* (pp. 41–68). Cambridge: Cambridge University Press.

BLEY-VROMAN, R.W., FELIX, S. and IOUP, G.L. 1988, The accessibility of Universal Grammar in adult language learning. *Second Language Research* 4 (1), 1–32.

BORER, H. and WEXLER, K. 1987, The maturation of syntax. In T. ROEPER and E. WILLIAMS (eds) *Parameter Setting* (pp. 123–87). Dordrecht: Reidel.

BURLING, R. 1959, Language development of a Garo and English speaking child. *Word* 15, 45–68.

CHOMSKY, N. 1989, Some notes on economy of derivation and representation. *MIT Working Papers in Linguistics* 10, 43–74.

CLYNE, M.G. 1977, Bilingualism of the elderly. *Talanya* 4, 45–56.

COOK, V.J. 1986, Experimental approaches applied to two areas of second language learning research: Age and listening-based teaching methods. In V.J. COOK (ed.) *Experimental Approaches to Second Language Learning* (pp. 23–37). Oxford: Pergamon.

— 1991, The poverty of the stimulus argument and multi-competence. *Second Language Research* 7 (2), 103–17.

— 1992, Evidence for multi-competence. *Language Learning* 42 (4), 557–91.

— 1993, *Linguistics and Second Language Acquisition*. Basingstoke: Macmillan.
— 1994, The metaphor of access to Universal Grammar. In N. ELLIS (ed.) *Implicit Learning and Language*. New York: Academic Press.
COOK, V.J., and NEWSON, M. (forthcoming), *Chomsky's Universal Grammar* (2nd edn). Oxford: Blackwell.
DE HOUWER, A. 1990, *The Acquisition of Two Languages from Birth: A Case Study*. Cambridge: Cambridge University Press.
DI SCIULLO, A-M., MUYSKEN, P. and SINGH, R. 1986, Government and code-mixing. *Journal of Linguistics* 22, 1–24.
FANTINI, A. 1985, *Language Acquisition of a Bilingual Child*. Battleboro: The Experiment Press.
GASSER, M. 1990, Connectionism and universals of second language acquisition. *Studies in Second Language Acquisition* 12 (2), 179–200.
GENESEE, F. 1989, Early bilingual development: One language or two? *Journal of Child Language* 16, 161–79.
GROSJEAN, F. 1989, Neurolinguists, beware! The bilingual is not two monolinguals in one person. *Brain and Language* 36, 3–15.
HALLIDAY, M.A.K., McINTOSH, A. and STREVENS, P. 1964, *The Linguistic Sciences and Language Teaching*. London: Longman
JOHNSON, J.S. and NEWPORT, E.L. 1991, Critical period effects on universal properties of languages: The status of subjacency in the acquisition of a second language. *Cognition* 39, 215–58.
KRASHEN, S., LONG, M. and SCARCELLA, R. 1979, Accounting for child–adult differences in second language rate and attainment. *TESOL Quarterly* 13, 573–82.
LEOPOLD, W.F. 1939–1949, *Speech Development of a Bilingual Child: A Linguist's Record: Volume I, Vocabulary Growth in the First Two Years; Volume II, Sound Learning in the First Two Years; Volume III, Grammar and General Problem in the First Two Years; Volume IV, Diary from Age Two*. Evanston: Northwestern University Press.
McLAUGHLIN, B. 1984, *Second Language Acquisition in Childhood: Volume I Pre-school Children*. New Jersey: Erlbaum.
McNEILL, D. 1966, Developmental psycholinguistics. In F. SMITH and G. MILLER (eds) *The Genesis of Language* (pp. 15–84). Cambridge, MA: MIT Press.
MEISEL, J.M. (ed.) 1990a, *Two First Languages: Early Grammatical Development in Bilingual Children*. Dordrecht: Foris.
— 1990b, Early differentiation of languages in bilingual children. In K. HYLTENSTAM and L.K. OBLER (eds) *Bilingualism Across the Lifespan* (pp. 13–40). Cambridge: Cambridge University Press.
MYERS-SCOTTON, C. 1992, Constructing the frame in intrasentential code-switching. *Multilingua* 11, 101–27.
NATHAN, G.S. 1987, On second-language acquisition of voiced stops. *Journal of Phonetics* 15, 313–22.
NEUFELD, G. 1978, On the acquisition of prosodic and articulatory features in adult language learning. *Canadian Modern Language Review* 34, 163–74.
OKSAAR, E. 1970, Zum Spacherwerb des Kindes in Zweisprachiger Umgebung. *Folia Linguistica* 4, 330–58.
OUHALLA, J. 1991, *Functional Categories and Parametric Variation*. London: Routledge.

OYAMA, S. 1976, A sensitive period for the acquisition of of a non-native phonological system. *Journal of Psycholinguistic Research* 5, 261–85.

PHILLIPSON, R. 1992, *Linguistic Imperialism*. Oxford: Oxford University Press.

POLLOCK, J.Y. 1989, Verb movement, universal grammar, and the structure of IP. *Linguistic Inquiry* 20, 365–424.

ROMAINE, S. 1989, *Bilingualism*. Oxford: Blackwell.

RONJAT, J. 1913, *Le développement du langage observé chez un enfant bilingue*. Paris: Champion.

RUKE-DRAVINA, V. 1967, *Mehrsprachigkeit im Vorschulalter*. Lund: Gleerup.

SCHACHTER, J. 1988, Second language acquisition and its relationship to Universal Grammar. *Applied Linguistics* 9 (3), 219–35.

SELIGER, H., KRASHEN, S. and LADEFOGED, P. 1975, Maturational constraints in the acquisition of second languages. *Language Sciences* 38, 20–2.

SELINKER, L. (1972), Interlanguage. *International Review of Applied Linguistics* 10, 209–31. Reprinted in J.C. RICHARDS (ed.) *Error Analysis* (pp. 31–54). London: Longman.

SINGLETON, D. 1989, *Language Acquisition: The Age Factor*. Clevedon: Multilingual Matters.

SOKOLIK, M.E. and SMITH, M.E. 1992, Assignment of gender to French nouns in primary and secondary language: A connectionist model. *Second Language Research* 8 (1), 39–58.

SRIDHAR, K.K. and SRIDHAR, S.N. 1986, Bridging the paradigm gap: Second language acquisition theory and indigenized varieties of English. *World Englishes* 5 (1), 3–14.

SWAIN, M. and WESCHE, M. 1975, Linguistic interaction: Case story of a bilingual child. *Language Sciences* 37, 17–22.

TABOURET-KELLER, A. 1962, L'acquisition du langage parlé chez un petit enfant en milieu bilingue. *Problèmes de Psycho-linguistiques* 8, 205–19.

TAESCHNER, T. 1983, *The Sun is Feminine*. Berlin: Springer.

VIHMAN, M.M. 1982, The acquisition of morphology by a bilingual child. *Applied Psycholinguistics* 3, 141–60.

VOLTERRA, V. and TAESCHNER, T. 1978, The acquisition and development of language by bilingual children. *Journal of Child Language* 5 (2), 311–26.

WEXLER, K. and MANZINI, M.R. 1987, Parameters and learnability. In T. ROEPER and E.WILLIAMS (eds) *Parameters and Linguistic Theory*. Dordrecht: Reidel.

3 Some Critical Remarks Concerning Penfield's Theory of Second Language Acquisition

HANS W. DECHERT

Introduction

In recent years an ever-increasing appreciation of the dynamics and complexity of second language acquisition phenomena has become a shared experience in the literature. A theory of second language acquisition no longer appears so easy (Klein, 1990). This means that certain hypotheses, such as the Critical Period Hypothesis, or certain 'Models', derived from assumed basic paradigms or elementary mechanisms, have turned out to be fatally oversimplified and thus obsolete. Unfortunately, the discussion of the practical consequences of such hypothetical constructs over the years has dominated the field and has undoubtedly had a significant influence on far-reaching political decisions: language planning, the production of teaching materials, methodological discussion, and the actual teaching of modern languages — especially in primary education.

The acquisition of language, be it first or second, is a fascinating, but also an extremely complex, phenomenon whose course and final result are determined by a number of interacting factors. The serious researcher in this field should carefully explore the full range of this process, try to isolate the various factors which govern it, characterize the way in which these factors interact, and eventually develop a theory which is able to explain it. In doing so, it is important to have an eye on what people in related fields think and claim about language and about human cognition in general. But this view should not be taken for granted. Jumping on the bandwagon of other disciplines which at present enjoy more scientific glamor will not get us closer to a theory

> of language acquisition. We should be modest enough to admit that at present we are still very far from such a theory, and proud enough to consider our work an independent and substantial contribution to a better understanding of language and human cognition. (Klein, 1990: 230f.)

If this makes sense today, it follows that the decomposition of the complexity of language acquisition, in a continuous striving by various experts from various fields — glamorous and peripheral — to isolate the individual interacting factors, promises only to prepare the ground for an even more disparate set of theoretical foundations for language acquisition research practice. We need, in particular, to be on our guard against any unjustified blend of levels of conceptualization (see Part 1 of Appendix 3.1). Attempts at solutions based on reductionism and overgeneralization will not spirit away the complexity of language perception and production. Thus, for example, the identification, location and description of the physical 'causes' of mental events do not constitute grounds for a claim that one understands the events in question. There is and remains a gap between the 'neuro' disciplines — neurology, neurobiology, neurophysiology, etc. — and the 'psycho' disciplines — psychology of language, psycholinguistics, etc. Not to mention the gap between both these areas and what is widely regarded as linguistics proper. Witelson puts it thus:

> The reductionist view that knowledge of the neurobiological underpinnings of behavior explains the behavioral entity itself is clearly simplistic. (Witelson, 1987: 653)

What is needed then is a componential approach which does not confuse the respective levels of analysis and description. To quote Witelson again:

> The study of brain–behavior relationships may help to elucidate the mental process itself. For example the study of amnesic patients has dramatically dissected memory into dissociable components...strongest support of a hypothesis may come from converging evidence from different approaches. (Witelson, 1987: 654)

To avoid any possible misunderstanding, it should perhaps be stated explicitly that we have no difficulty in agreeing with researchers such as Jacobs and Schumann that an approach is required which integrates the neurosciences, an approach exemplified by Penfield's work many years ago:

> Research that extrapolates mental metaphors from observed behaviour must be supplemented and constrained by a neurally inspired paradigm that attempts to understand behavior based on the structure of

> the organ from which all behavior originates: the brain. (Jacobs & Schumann, 1992: 295)

However, we insist that it must always be borne in mind that there is a necessity 'for multiple explanations of complex phenomena at different levels of fineness of detail' (Simon, 1979: 62), and we argue that these levels must not be blended but need to be kept separate in order that they may be analysed and described appropriately.

The Construction of a Metaphorical Analogue Model

The discussion that follows continues the line taken in the Introduction in suggesting that a theory of language acquisition, *any* theory of language acquisition, will be far from easy to formulate and that such a theory must be componential. Accordingly, the thematic scope of this article will be undeniably a narrowly limited one: *some critical remarks* concerning Penfield's theory of *second* language acquisition. For this reason it will as far as possible avoid reference to Penfield's neuroscientific work and attempt to focus mainly on three of his publications (Penfield, 1953; Penfield & Roberts, 1959; Penfield, 1965; see Appendixes 32, 33 and 3.4), in which he developed a theory of language acquisition or at least referred to theoretical dimensions of language acquisition. They also comprise that part of his work on which his fame as an advocate of primary-level second language programmes is based.

The Appendixes to this chapter set out to document parts of the original material which exemplifies his way of theorising. In selecting and combining these passages and early critical reviews of Penfield's work, it is our intention to cast doubt on some of Penfield's theoretical positions by quoting him as well as critical statements of some reviewers of high status. These reviewers are, of course, Penfield's own contemporaries. From our present state of knowledge of the state of the art, to be sure, none of the hypotheses advocated in the three texts (Penfield, 1953; Penfield & Roberts, 1959; Penfield, 1965), with the exception of Hypothesis 6, may be considered to have firm enough foundations to constitute unassailable hard-science bases for the Critical Age Hypothesis. But this is not the focus of this paper, which proposes, rather, a reflection on the inconsistencies in Penfield's own theorising in terms of his own time.

What does a researcher do who wants to make his/her new discoveries known to the public and to draw conclusions in respect of the revision of certain practices that he/she may no longer subscribe to in the light of his/her knowledge? What is the manifestation of such discoveries in his/her own life story? He/she is likely to look for or to construct an analogue model which one way or the other resembles the structure of the problem that seems to be better understood and thus to be settled by the outcome of his/her reasoning.

It is interesting to note that in the three articles in question (Penfield, 1953; Penfield & Roberts, 1959; Penfield, 1965) Penfield refers to a biographical event which must not only have made a deep impression on him but must have had a remarkable explanatory power for him. It presents a sort of gestalt-like metaphor in his attempt at analogically modelling his theorising of the linguistic representation of objects in the world and as such an iconic case of units of language.

The following quotation is taken from the 1953 lecture (p. 202; cf. also Penfield & Roberts, 1959: 239):

> Speaking, and the understanding of speech, also reading and writing depend upon the employment of certain specialized areas of the cerebrum. ...In the history of our race, we know little of the beginnings of speech. It has been said that it was when man learned to cultivate grain in the valleys of the Nile and the Euphrates that the birth of civilization was made possible. But there was a more important prerequisite to that civilization — the learning of language. The writing of that language came later, and its evolution can be traced in the tablets of Mesopotamia.

And immediately following is the life story narrative that connects the preceding arguments with the 'story of writing', which serves to establish coherence and to provide anecdotal evidence which then is immediately turned into 'hard science' neurological argumentation!

> I remember a day when I stepped out of the blazing sun of a street in Baghdad into the Iraq Museum. [Note the introductory function of describing the locale according to a story schema!] There, in the museum's half light, I saw rows of clay tablets, each of them shaped like a piece of soap. On them could be seen the stages in the story of writing from picture-drawing and counting to alphabet. Seton Lloyd, then Curator of the Museum, picked up a tablet and held it in the palm of his hand just as some Sumerian scribe must have held it when it was soft clay more than 5000 years ago. He pointed out the pictograph of a bag of barley and the single mark of the stylus which stood for the number ten (the number of a man's fingers) and the different marks which were used to represent ones. Here was a record of sale at a time when man had learned to cultivate grain in that fertile plain, a time when speech was probably quite well developed and when man was

> about to turn from pictograph to writing, an evolution which seems to have been relatively rapid.

And at once following, almost fulfilling the function of a coda:

> Today we have learned to understand something of the cerebral mechanisms which enable man to speak [which the book is about], and later to write and read. I shall describe these in simple outline [*sic*!].

What does this episode stand for? As Penfield admits, 'we know little of the beginnings of speech', and therefore there is very little to be said in his narrative; he nevertheless turns to the period preceding the origin and history of written language as documented in the museum before coming back to the topic of speech, which is the subject of this lecture and article.

> But there was a more important prerequisite to that civilization — the learning of language. The writing of that language came later, and its evolution can be traced in the tablets of Mesopotamia.

There can be no doubt that the Baghdad episode has significance for Penfield, mainly in his discussion of speech development and teaching.

One of the implications of this analogy becomes evident in two later passages in the same 1953 article:

> I spoke of the discovery of writing in Sumer 5000 years and more ago. Semitic conquerors soon came into Sumer speaking a language which we might call Babylonian. They were warlike and untutored. They had much to learn from the more ancient civilization of Sumer. The temple libraries of that land and in that period were filled with clay tablets written in the Sumerian tongue.
>
> Gradually, the common language in city and country came to be Babylonian, but contracts, decisions at law and bills of sale were still invariably written in Sumerian. Educated people understood both tongues. (Penfield, 1953: 209)

And half a page later:

> But times have changed and with them the learning of a secondary language. The Babylonian once bought a Sumerian slave to teach his children, at an early age, a tongue that would be useful to them when they grew up to become priests, merchants, courtiers... In more recent times, governesses and maids who spoke foreign tongues could be hired, and this may well be possible in some parts of the world still. But slavery is gone and domestic servants seem to be fast disappearing on this continent.

> The time has come to establish new methods of learning the secondary languages. (Penfield, 1953: 210)

It is not the early history of writing that constitutes the prime motivation in the reconstruction of the Baghdad episode in the 1953 Boston lecture; it is rather the story of the interaction of languages and the acquisition of secondary languages, taught by slaves, maids and governesses, that is of particular significance. In different contexts Penfield talks about the linguistic history of his own children — in contradistinction to his own linguistic history — which actually is the only anecdotal evidence he adduces for the early introduction of second languages into the primary school curriculum. The particular way of early second language teaching that he advocates, 'the direct method that mothers use', was, he claims 'used in the families of ancient Ur' (1965: 792). That is to say, 12 years after the recounting of the Baghdad narrative, 'ancient Ur' has remained the analogue model for early language learning. This is the biographical reason for the blend between the history of writing (as exhibited in the Baghdad Museum) and the reconstructed oral acquisition of (first and) secondary languages in Mesopotamia (only implicitly documented in the Baghdad Museum), but experientially observed in the linguistic history of his children, as opposed to his own language learning experience.

The Baghdad Museum narrative and the passages referring to it serve as a metaphorical analogue model for Penfield's theorising about early language acquisition. It is based on a blend between oral and written language, and attempts to exhibit historical depth to anecdotal evidence experienced in his own familiar context.

The second implication of the metaphorical analogue model constructed as a consequence of the Baghdad event is found in the *Tabula Rasa* Hypothesis. At the beginning of the 1953 paper (Penfield, 1953: 201), just one page before the introduction of the Baghdad event, the slate metaphor, a particular instantiation of the *tabula rasa* metaphor, is used:

> When a baby comes into the world the speech areas of the cerebral cortex are like a clean slate, ready to be written upon [*sic*!].

In the course of the subsequent account of the Baghdad event, the clay tablets presented to the narrator (Penfield) by the museum's curator are described as documents 'of the story of writing' upon which first pictographs and then representational information were written. 'The writing of that language', 'traced in tablets', came after the learning of the language.

The history of speaking followed by the history of writing is nothing else but the metaphorical analogue model of the ontogenetic development of (first and second) language acquisition as inferred from the visit to the Baghdad Museum and described immediately following the Baghdad narrative:

> When a child begins to speak, there develops a functional specialisation in one cerebral hemisphere. ...There are separate areas of the cortex on...the dominant side which come to be devoted to the formulation and the understanding of speech. Meanwhile the slate continues to be blank on the right side. (Penfield, 1953: 203)

Whereas the slate on the dominant side, in other words, is written upon, the slate of the non-dominant side remains empty. This ontogenetic analogue to the history of speaking and writing in the narration of the Baghdad event is the answer to the introductory passage connecting the narrative with the argumentational passage already quoted:

> Today we have learned to understand something of the cerebral mechanisms which enable man to begin to speak, and later to write and read. I shall describe these in simple outline. (Penfield, 1953: 203)

This 'simple outline' is derived from the second inference from the metaphorical analogue model. The 'soft clay tablets' in the Baghdad Museum, originally clean slates to be written upon, are the analogues of the neural *tabula rasa*, one of the basic epistemological axioms of British empiricism to which Penfield quite obviously adheres. As far as language is concerned, these neural clean slates will be written upon with the units of language to be perceived. Penfield's notion of 'speech mechanism' is thus clearly influenced by the *Tabula Rasa* Hypothesis:

> The infant possesses a speech mechanism, but it is only a potential mechanism. It is a clean slate, waiting for what that infant is to hear and see, ...language will serve as the vehicle for practically all forms of knowledge. (Penfield & Roberts, 1959: 238)

The *Tabula Rasa* Hypothesis finally serves as the physiological foundation for the Critical Age Hypothesis. The Babylonian clay tablet notion blends with the *Tabula Rasa* Hypothesis in the description of the historical process from oral speech to written language according to which the soft clay tablets were used to carry the written presentation of the orally transmitted message as a stage in the development of writing:

> Before the child begins to speak and to perceive, the uncommitted cortex is a blank slate on which nothing has been written. In the ensuing years much is written, and the writing is normally never erased. After the age of ten or twelve, the general functional connexions have been established and fixed for the speech cortex. After that, the speech centre

> cannot be transferred to the cortex of the lesser side and set up all over again. This 'non-dominant' area that might have been used for speech is now fully occupied with the business of perception. (Penfield, 1965: 792)

The *Tabula Rasa* Hypothesis operates thus in an ontogenetic perspective: the full use of the dominant committed part of the cortex leads to an irreversible functional fixation of speech production and speech perception and no longer allows other options. This is the logical basis for the Critical Age Hypothesis.

The Construction of a Metaphorical Notion of 'Unit'

In the final chapter of the 1959 volume, devoted to the learning of language, a central notion of Penfield's theorising, the notion of 'unit' is hypothesised and discussed.

> Man has inherited the motor mechanisms which make speaking possible. But there is no inheritance of those things that he adds to his ideational speech mechanism while he is learning a language. The clean blank speech slate which he brought with him into the world is soon filled with units, and after the first decade of life they can hardly be erased. They can be added to, but with increasing difficulty. (Penfield & Roberts, 1959: 250f.)

Experientially perceived units of information that fill the *tabula rasa* speech slate during the course of language acquisition! What are these 'units' like?

In a special paragraph explicitly focused on the 'brain-mechanisms of language', Penfield attempts to answer this question. Children, when they learn to speak, must establish and store neuronal records of the concepts whose names they learn, and, at the same time, they must establish neuronal records of these concepts themselves. Between the two, the neuronal record of the concept and the neuronal record of the name, a connection — a reflex — must be established. The pattern of this neuronal connection makes up a 'unit' as well. Conceptualisation, naming, memorising, speaking and perceiving the word that is the realisation of the name constitute a verbal 'unit'. If such a unit is articulated, it is a motor unit.

> ...when the child begins to understand, he is establishing general *concept-units* in the brain and corresponding *word-sound-units*. When he begins to speak he must establish *word-formation-units*. During this early experimental period he uses his voluntary motor system to make a more and more accurate sound, thus correcting and reinforcing the image of how to speak the word. What I called an *image* is really a

> pattern of the motor complex required to produce the *word*. This *image* or *motor-pattern* is a unit, too, and the neurones involved in the pattern-unit are clearly located in the speech areas. (Penfield & Roberts, 1959: 247; my emphasis)

We gather that the concept of 'unit' in this passage is a fuzzy one, a problem not uncommonly run into by various scientific attempts to introduce strategies for theory assessment (cf. Darden, 1991). It is true that the following quotation appears to throw a clearer light on Penfield's conceptualisation, but again what emerges is a somewhat disagreeable oversimplification.

> Thus, man is able to find, in his ideational speech mechanism, four sets of neurone patterns: the *sound units of words* employed when listening to speech, the *verbal units* followed for speaking, the *visual units* for reading, and the *manual units* for writing. (Penfield & Roberts, 1959: 250; my emphasis)

It is true that the four units resemble the four skills and thus are not restricted to speech production (the topic of the 1959 volume), but they can hardly be regarded as an expansion in the direction of a componential theory of first and second language acquisition.

The theme of second languages is dealt with in a special paragraph under that particular heading in Penfield & Roberts's 1959 volume. In this paragraph the notion of 'unit' is further discussed and three methods of second language learning are distinguished: (i) the indirect method, (ii) the direct method, and (iii) the mother's method.

Little needs to be said about (i).

> In the indirect method the learner 'employs the units which were fixed in his speech mechanism in childhood. Thus, he begins to translate, and there is set up a new neurophysiological process: *indirect language learning*.' (Penfield & Roberts, 1959: 252)

According to this method the teacher (if his/her second language happens to be French, and English the student's mother tongue) instructs them 'to speak French with units that belong to the English tongue' (p. 252). Needless to say, this method is to be blamed.

In exercising the direct method (ii) the same mechanism 'is developed in the brain whether one, two, or more languages are learned'. According to this method,

> ...a child who is exposed to two or three languages...pronounces each with the accent of his teacher. If he hears one language at home, another at school, and a third, perhaps, with a governess in the nursery, he is

> not aware that he is learning three languages at all. He is aware of the fact that to get what he wants with the governess he must speak one way, and with his teacher he must speak in another way. He does not reason it out at all. There is no French, no German, no English. It is simpler than that. (Penfield & Roberts, 1959: 253)

So there is no language awareness, no metacognition, no transfer, no cognition! This remark is just to show the narrowness of Penfield's argumentation in the light of our present knowledge.

As to the mother's method (iii), in Penfield's terms the most favourable one,

> ...one secret of the success of this method is, of course, that it is employed while a child is forming the speech units in his eager little brain. A child who hears three languages instead of one, early enough, learns the units of all three without added effort and without confusion. (Penfield & Roberts, 1959: 254)

In the foregoing discussion of Penfield's notion of unit and the various connotations attached to it, it should have become evident that it may be seen as an attempt to introduce a concept representing an enormously complex phenomenon, a characteristic step in the early assessment and treatment of new phenomena in the history of science. The consensus today would probably be that first and second language acquisition cannot be described by a separable notion of 'unit', which is on the one hand oversimplified and on the other highly ambiguous. This notion is, as we try to indicate in our Appendix, in fact severely criticised in two critical reviews by eminent reviewers of Penfield's own time. What is proposed in these reviews is a complication of the simplified notions of unit and a more sophisticated approach to theorising *vis-à-vis* second language acquisition.

The obvious vagueness of the term 'unit', if it makes sense at all, certainly needs clearer definition and further expansion — as we have tried to argue in our references below to the work of Milner and Hebb. What is first of all needed, though, is a more substantial theory-constitutive metaphor. And, to be sure, in spite of the long tradition in aphasiology, it is not the word, but larger or different stretches of speech (perhaps speech 'fragments' in Milner's terms) which are the true units of speech processing (cf. Peters 1983; Fillmore 1976). The upshot of the above discussion would appear to be that hard science methodology and argumentation will, unless corroborated by linguistic, psycholinguistic and sociolinguistic argumentation, lead us astray in our attempts to deal with the complex questions to be assessed in a componential effort towards a complex theory of language acquisition.

Conclusion

In the light of our present knowledge about second language acquisition and the various still insufficient contributions made by different approaches referring to different contexts and differingly distant languages to a componential theory of language acquisition, there can be no doubt that children at an early age, especially in natural contexts, but also in tutored contexts, can learn and do learn secondary languages. Multicompetence at an early age is possible. More than that, it is desirable.

It is equally evident that older children, adolescents and adults too may and do learn secondary languages in natural and tutored contexts. Multicompetence is also possible for these age-groups. Again, more than that, it is desirable. Indeed, one might argue that it is especially desirable for these age-groups.

It is clear that there are more people in the world who are multicompetent one way or another than who are monocompetent. A further increase in multicompetence will hopefully contribute to a deeper understanding among people and peoples in this world. In the light of our present knowledge — and this is a different story — we do not know whether there is a critical age or a series of critical ages which *only* or *mainly* on a sound scientific basis would justify an institutionally motivated introduction of early primary second language teaching. Much too little is known about its advantages, which certainly do exist, and its disadvantages, which exist as well.

What this article argues for is the need for substantial theory-guided evidence across various fields of research towards a componential theory of early or later second language acquisition. What it criticises is assumed hard science evidence.

Appendix 3.1

Herbert A. Simon (1976) The information-storage system called 'human memory'. In Mark R. Rosenzweig and Edward L. Bennett (eds) *Neural Mechanisms of Learning and Memory* (pp. 79–96). Cambridge, MA: The MIT Press. Reprinted in Herbert A. Simon (ed.) (1979) *Models of Thought* (pp. 62–83). New Haven: Yale University Press.

Information Processing and Physiological Approaches

> There are numerous examples in modern science of the need for multiple explanations of complex phenomena at different levels of fineness of detail. (p. 62)

> We see the natural world as an immensely complex hierarchical system, understandable only by being represented alternatively at many levels of detail, and understood by constructing bodies of theory at each of these levels, in combination with reduction theories that show how the unanalyzed elementary structures at each level can themselves be explained in terms of the constructs available at the next level below. (p. 63)
>
> The symbol structures and elementary information processes of information processing psychology must therefore have their physiological counterparts in subsystems within the central nervous system that function as memory units, and subsystems that are capable of processing these physiologically stored structures. The term 'system' is used here rather than 'unit' to avoid commitment to any assumption of localism — any notion that each symbol structure that is stored must have its specific storage location in the brain. Nothing in contemporary information processing theories of memory requires that memories be specifically localized; and nothing in those theories is incompatible with a distributed or even holographic theory of the physiological basis for memory. (p. 64)
>
> To achieve the kind of explanation of human cognition that we want to and need to have, we will have to construct an information processing theory to handle the complex phenomena, a bridge theory to show how the primitive structures and processes of the theory are realized physiologically, and a physiological theory to show what the basic biological and biochemical mechanisms are that implement the physiological functions. (p. 64)

Appendix 3.2

Wilder [Graves] Penfield (1953) (Department of Neurology and Neurosurgery, McGill University, and the Montreal Neurological Institute) A consideration of the neurophysiological mechanisms of speech and some educational consequences. Paper read at the 1364th meeting at the American Academy of Arts and Sciences, Boston, February 11, 1953. *Proceedings of the American Academy of Arts and Sciences* 82 (5), 201–3.

In a footnote (p. 203) the following additional information is given anticipating the publication of Penfield & Roberts (1959):

> At the present time, Dr Lamar Roberts and the writer are analyzing about 575 such cases [of local interference in the cortex] in a study to appear shortly. We have had the help of Mr R.W. Sparks, speech therapist. An earlier study of such cases was made by Dr Preston Robb,

and those in which the frontal lobe was involved were published (1948). Penfield and Rasmussen have recorded evidence regarding vocalisation and arrest of speech (1949; also 1950).

In the Penfield & Roberts (1959) volume, according to the case index (p. 281), provided by Anne Dawson, Executive Secretary of the Montreal Institute, only 34 cases are listed. These are the cases discussed in the volume. In the Penfield & Roberts (1959) volume (p. 236) the authors recall the Boston lecture and the reaction, especially that of the Modern Languages Association of America.

In the presentation to the meeting of the American Academy of Arts and Sciences at Boston, Penfield outlines the axiomatic foundation of his research concerning the acquisition of native and foreign speech:

The *Tabula Rasa* Hypothesis

> Man has spoken language which must be taught to each growing child. His ability to learn to speak depends upon the postnatal organisation of speech mechanisms within his brain. When a baby comes into the world the speech areas of the cerebral cortex are like a clean slate, ready to be written upon. (p. 201)

The Optimum Age Hypothesis

> Speaking, and the understanding of speech, also reading and writing, depend upon the employment of certain specialized areas of the cerebrum. There is an optimum age... (p. 202)

In the concrete delimitation of this age in later portions of the text Penfield is rather vague:

> If, before the age of 10 or 14, the child associates with those who speak a second and even a third language, he can learn by a similar technique [to the mother's method of teaching his first language] two or three languages with no evident increase in his effort. (p. 207)

Compare:

> Let the first years, from nursery school and kindergarten on to grades for children of eight or ten, be conducted by foreign-born teachers... (p. 211)

The Plasticity Hypothesis

> There is an optimum age when these special areas [of the cerebrum responsible for speaking] are plastic and receptive... (p. 202)

The Lateralisation Hypothesis

> When a child begins to speak, there develops a functional specialization in one cerebral hemisphere, normally the left hemisphere... There are separate areas of the cortex on this, the dominant side which come to be devoted to the formulation and the understanding of speech. Meanwhile the slate continues to be blank on the right side. (p. 203)

And in a later context:

> But, once functional localization of acquired skills has been established, the early plasticity tends to disappear. (p. 206)

The Switch-Mechanism (or Avoidance of Interference) Hypothesis

> If languages are learned in the right way, and particularly if they are learned at the right age, multiple languages may be learned perfectly, with little effort and without physiological confusion. (p. 209)

The Multicompetence Hypothesis

> There is a good deal of evidence that he who learns more than one language as a little child has greater facility for the acquisition of additional languages in adult life. (p. 212)

The 'Hard' Science Hypothesis

In spite of the author's explicit recognition of the constraints of his approach as a neurologist ('I make no pretence to knowledge of the best organization of such a school [in which languages are taught appropriately]' (p. 212)), he over and over again claims to be able to present the true scientific theoretical frame of reference for questioning 'the pseudo-scientific discussion' among educators, that is, the 'accepted methods of teaching foreign language' (p. 202).

> Today we have learned to understand something of the cerebral mechanisms which enable man to begin to speak, and later to write and read. (p. 203)

As to the 'educational consequences' announced in the title of the address, that is, an alternative proposal for the teaching of foreign languages following from his neurological considerations, Penfield clearly states:

> In the observations which follow it is my purpose to question the accepted methods of teaching foreign language. I venture to do this, not because I claim any specialized knowledge of pedagogy... (p. 202)

In a later passage he is even more outspoken:

> More than once I have heard from an assistant, who was well versed in the published literature on this subject [bilingualism], that an aphasic patient could speak French but was aphasic in English or vice versa. On critical examination it always developed that both languages were involved in the speech defect. (p. 208)

It seems that the hypotheses mentioned so far demand a theoretical justification or empirical evidence if they are to be considered seriously — not, to be sure, in terms of our present knowledge, but in terms of the knowledge available at the time of the conceptualisations that underlie this text. Here is Penfield's response to this requirement as given in the Boston lecture:

> I had the opportunity of watching this experiment [relative to the question of whether a child before the age of 10 or 14 can learn two or three languages with no evident increase in his effort in the natural way] carried out in my own home. Two of our children spoke German in the nursery with a German governess from the beginning. Then, when they first went to school it was to a French nursery school at the ages of 3 and 4. There, work and play were presented to them in the French tongue.
>
> In the nursery with the governess it seemed to them quite natural that the word for dog was 'hund'. In the nursery school it was 'chien' and when they were with their parents it was 'dog'. There was no confusion, no extra effort, no foreign accents. The change in environment was sufficient to change the way of expression. Or the appearance of the governess who never spoke anything but German might have the same result. The parents also spoke German to the best of their ability in the nursery. This established what might be considered a conditioned reflex.
>
> The experiment was successful. Even the two older children who had played with German children for only a few months at the ages of 9 and 10 continued to talk with the German governess who entered the family at the time. In each case fluent command of the language was achieved without labor, and the ability has since served useful purposes to three of the four children. (p. 207)

The veracity of these narratives is not in question. But was this really an 'experiment', and is the evidence it provides really more than anecdotal? Does it really have the scientific credentials presupposed by Hypothesis 7?

Appendix 3.3

Wilder [Graves] Penfield and Lamar Roberts (1959) *Speech and Brain Mechanisms*. Princeton, NJ: Princeton University Press.

The imprint on the reverse of the title page gives the following information on the academic status of both authors:

> Dr Wilder Penfield has been Director of the Montreal Neurological Institute since its founding in 1934, and is Chairman of the Department of Neurology and Neurosurgery of McGill University. He holds the Order of Merit from the British Crown, and honorary degrees from 17 universities, including the two at which he was once an undergraduate: Princeton and Oxford.
>
> Among the learned societies of which he is a fellow or member are the National Academy of Sciences of the US and of the USSR, the Royal Society of London, the Académie Nationale de Médecine, France, and the American Philosophical Society.
>
> He has previously published six books on various phases of neurology, neurosurgery, and neurophysiology, and is at present working on an historical novel that deals with Hippocrates.
>
> Dr Lamar Roberts is Chief of Neurosurgery at the University of Florida Medical School. After earning his doctorate in medicine at Duke University, he was awarded the MSc and PhD degrees at McGill University for his graduate studies on speech defects and neurological localization.

There can be no doubt that the tremendous influence, particularly of Penfield, in the propagation of second language programmes in primary schools is to a large extent due to his outstanding career as a neurologist (cf. Singleton, 1989: 234f.).

The Preface of the volume outlines (p. vii) the genesis of the book and its goal:

> This book is the outcome of ten years of carefully planned study of brain dominance, and of aphasia and other speech disturbances. It is a discussion of the cerebral mechanisms of speech, the learning of language. ...Our initial aim was to present this evidence [from the study of various cases researched at the Neurological Institute] in monograph form, together with a review of the literature. This we have done. Our further intention was to make as clear a statement as we could of the neurophysiology of language and to locate its mechanisms. We have made a beginning on this second task. But hypothetical reasoning must always wait on the tests of time. And if, in the end, our

> hypotheses are found wanting, they should serve nonetheless to guide other explorers who pass this way. Psychologists may well find as much useful material in this monograph as the clinicians and the neurophysiologists for whom it was originally intended. The fundamentals of speech mechanisms discussed here should help speech therapists.

It seems that Penfield's own recommendation that his statements be considered as hypothetical, that is lacking empirical evidence, has been overlooked by many of his readers (if he was ever carefully read at all by those who used his statements as a justification for their own educational goals). This must be said to be fair to Penfield!

The Preface continues (p. vii) with the mention of the oral presentation of the material:

> The parts of the material suitable to a general university audience were used in the Vanuxem Lectures at Princeton University in 1956. That presentation modified inevitably the treatment of the evidence. Consequently a final chapter entitled *The Learning of Languages* has been added that may interest educators and the teachers of modern languages.

> As the enumeration of Vanuxem Lecturers (p. ix) between 1912 and 1958 discloses, this lecture series has associated with it a large number of highly prestigious names — names such as F.C. Bartlett, J.R. Oppenheimer, Dylan Thomas, K.S. Lashley, W. Köhler, J. von Neumann and K. Lorenz.

The volume contains 11 chapters, five written by Roberts and six written by Penfield:

1. Introduction (WP)
2. Functional Organisation of the Human Brain, Discriminative Sensation, Voluntary Movement (WP)
3. The Recording of Consciousness and the Function of Interpretive Cortex (WP)
4. Analysis of Literature (LR)
5. Methods of Investigation (LR)
6. Handedness and Cerebral Dominance (LR)
7. Mapping the Speech Area (WP)
8. The Evidence from Cortical Mapping (LR)
9. The Evidence from Cortical Excision (LR)
10. Concluding Discussion (WP)
11. Epilogue: The Learning of Languages (WP)

The final chapter on which we have concentrated in the preceding discussion is ordered like this:

That is to say, about 20 pages out of 257 deal explicitly with 'the learning of languages', the topic relative to which this volume has been quoted over and over again, and only seven pages deal with the acquisition of second languages, which for about 40 years have served to justify the early introduction of secondary languages, in various countries, in accordance with the natural 'mother's method'!

A short look at two passages from the works of H.H. Stern, without any question for more than 30 years one of the most outstanding Canadian researchers in the second language learning/teaching field, may illustrate the tremendous influence of Penfield's recommendations. Under the heading 'Neurological Aspects' in the introductory chapter to his 1967 volume — a chapter entitled 'Arguments for Early Second Language Learning' — Stern writes (pp. 26f.):

> In the discussion on the merits and demerits of early language learning the opinion of the Canadian neurologist Wilder Penfield in favour of an early start received much prominence. ...Languages, he argues, should be learnt by 'the normal physiological process' as a by-product of other pursuits. The brain has a biological time-table of language learning. The complex speech mechanisms of the dominant hemisphere of the cerebral cortex develop in infancy and childhood before the onset of puberty. We must face the fact that the young organism

> has a capacity for the acquisition of new speech mechanisms which the adult no longer possesses to the same extent. Hence use ought to be made of this 'plasticity' of the brain in the early years, because for a young brain it is no more difficult to learn two or three languages than it is to learn one.
>
> Penfield bases these views primarily on the results of studies of brain damage at different stages of life: a child who has lost the use of one hemisphere and has become aphasic can relearn language; adults, he claims, do not have this capacity. He further cites psychological evidence of language achievement in childhood and the observations on the language development of his own children in a multilingual milieu.

Although one must not overlook the critical implications of this last paragraph as to the conceptual foundation of Penfield's point of view — and Stern does not hesitate to cite Milner's critical review of the Penfield & Roberts volume (Milner, 1960) — he finally fully agrees with Penfield in his own statement at the end of the chapter (p. 27):

> From a neurophysiological point of view there is no good reason against an early start: on the contrary, there are good positive indications for it. This is not to say, of course, that language learning — especially the conceptual aspects of language — may not be taken up successfully in later life. Educationists and psychologists should take more and more into account the findings of neurophysiology in this area

And even in his widely known volume *Fundamental Concepts of Language Teaching* (Stern, 1983) he does not revise this position in favour of Penfield:

> A psychological issue that began to be discussed in the fifties was the question of the optimal age for second language learning. The ability of young children to learn languages 'easily' had, from time to time, been noted in the psychological literature. ...But in the fifties it was the view of Penfield, a neurophysiologist at McGill University in Montreal, which aroused widespread attention. Penfield, partly on the basis of his scientific work as a neurosurgeon and partly on his personal conviction, put forward the idea that the early years before puberty offered a biologically favourable stage for second language learning, and he recommended that the early years of childhood should be used more intensively for language training. This viewpoint, shared by a growing number of teachers, specialists, and the general public, manifested itself in the introduction of language teaching in the early years of schooling in several countries. (Stern, 1983: 323)

Appendix 3.4

Wilder [Graves] Penfield (1965) Conditioning the uncommitted cortex for language learning. *Brain* 88, 787–98.

According to a footnote (p. 787), part of this article 'was published in different form in *The Atlantic Monthly* (1964) 214, p. 77 under the title *The Uncommitted Cortex*'.

According to another footnote (p. 793), Chapters 12 and 13 'of a more recent book' by Penfield, Little, Brown, published in Toronto 1963 [*sic*!], 'also deal with second language learning'. In spite of a bibliographical search we have not been able to exactly trace the title, publisher, location or year of this publication.

In this present article Penfield informs the reader of a 'series of two broadcasts over the All-India Radio on the teaching of secondary languages, given in 1957' (that is, seven years previously!). At that time 10,000 copies of this radio presentation were printed and distributed to Indian teachers. This episode seems to indicate that within a comparatively short period of time after the appearance of the *Proceedings of the American Academy of Arts and Sciences* in 1953, and even before the publication of *Speech and Brain Mechanisms* in 1959, Penfield to some extent must have had achieved a remarkable international reputation as an expert in modern language learning and teaching, at least among educators. This easily explains how it is that the 1965 article in *Brain* is 'intended for educators and parents, in the hope that it may help them to adjust school curricula and home instruction to the changing physiology of the brain of childhood' (p. 787).

Once again, arguments well known to us from the 1953 and 1959 texts, discussed earlier, serve to explain his motivation:

> The request [by the Indian Department of Education to talk about language pedagogy] was startling to me, not because the problem was new but because an educator had turned to a neurosurgeon.

And immediately following this hard science sort of justification for his expertise, the evidence problem is solved:

> My wife tried to reassure me by pointing out that our own children had gained a satisfactory command of two added languages. We had done no more than to have them hear German and French well-spoken in their early childhood. ...my own children learned to use German and French without apparent effort, without foreign accent, and without the long hours of toil that I had sacrificed to language study. They did well what I did badly. (p. 788)

Of particular interest in this connection is the short mention of his own foreign language acquisition history, which is to serve as negative evidence in support of the method he advocates. But, besides this, this episode from his life history undoubtedly has the function of an explanatory system which is to rationalise his own linguistic problems:

> For my own part, I had heard no foreign tongue before the age of 16. After that, I studied three modern languages for professional purposes but spoke none well. Before beginning the study of medicine, I even spent a whole year teaching German and was paid for it in an otherwise efficient boys' school. It was, I fear, very poor language teaching. I handed on, as best I could, the words and the grammar I had learned at Princeton to boys who were between 15 and 18 years of age. (p. 788)

His pupils, in other words, were years beyond the supposed optimum age. This obvious attempt to construct coherence through a critical account of his own linguistic socialisation, his failure as a second-language teacher of German to students after the critical age and the claim to have the scientific answer to the problem is obviously related to his astounding engagement in favour of a particular approach in language pedagogy, despite the absence of a sound theory of language acquisition. In coming to terms with the difference between his own L2 incompetence and his children's near-nativeness he reaches for a general physiological explanation — ignoring, of course, the possibility that his children might be more talented than their father!

In this connection it is revealing that immediately after that he turns to the Montreal context:

> I have had a remarkable opportunity to study speech mechanisms, language learning and bilingualism. Most of my clinical career has been passed in Montreal where my patients were, half of them, French-speaking and half English-speaking. (p. 788)

And as far as intelligence is concerned a few pages later:

> There is other good evidence that even a limited familiarity with additional languages in the first decade endows the normal child with a more efficient and useful brain. In a study supported by the Carnegie Foundation and conducted under W.E. Lambert, Professor of Psychology at McGill University, it was concluded recently that bilingual children, at the 10-year level in Montreal, showed greater intelligence than unilingual children of the same age. They were examined by non-verbal as well as verbal tests. (p. 797)

And finally in this connection, the following passage in which Canada (and Montreal) are not mentioned at all, although they were the real bilingual background of his own life story, deserves particular attention (cf. also Penfield & Roberts, 1959: 237, 251; Lambert, 1990: 203–10). Is it because he found true bilingualism there and felt himself to be excluded?

> There is a good deal of evidence to suggest that when a young child is allowed to hear a second language and learns to use only a few hundred words of that language — he becomes a better potential linguist; ... This would explain the reputed genius of the Swiss, the Poles and the Belgians as linguists. Most of them hear a second language in early childhood in the streets and the playgrounds, if not at home. On the contrary, the average so-called Anglo-Saxon, in Great Britain or the United States, hears only English until possibly he is taught a modern language in his teens at school. (p. 793)

Appendix 3.5

One of the most substantial, though comparatively short, reviews of *Speech and Brain Mechanisms* was by Peter M. Milner and appeared in 1960 in the *Canadian Journal of Psychology* (Milner, 1960). It is of particular interest insofar as Milner, a close associate of Donald Hebb's at McGill (cf. Milner, 1993), and a physiological psychologist himself, must not only have been in close personal contact with Penfield but have had insight into his work and his role in the Department of Psychology at McGill.

The review sets out with the psychological implications of speech processing and acquisition.

> *The problems of speech* enter into every branch of human psychology in one form or another. The acquisition of a language demands the ultimate in perceptual and motor learning: speech is intimately related to concept formation and thinking; verbal responses, once learned, are not forthcoming without motivation, and it is well known that words can be powerful arousers of motivation and emotion. Whether we read or listen, we receive information in small fragments which must be stored long enough to be perceived as words and sentences. In speaking and writing the reverse process must be carried through; the complex movements must be executed in definite sequences for the purpose of communicating a single idea. (Milner, 1960: 140f.)

If I am not mistaken, these few lines are indications of a much more complex and elaborated theory of language processing than the one developed in the review source book: Milner's insisting on psychology as the relevant science of theorising, the recognition of a combination of non-automatic and automatic processing, the allusion to a hierarchy of processing from conceptualisation down to verbalisation, the reference to the function of memory, the inclusion of mention of affective variables of language, the expansion from speech to written language and, above all, the introduction of a more elaborated unit of language processing ('we receive information in small fragments which must be stored long enough to be perceived as words and sentences'). It seems as if Donald Hebb's notion of larger neuronal units of cell assemblies has found its expression in Milner's conceptualisation of units of processing beyond the word unit. Milner's critical evaluation of Penfield's book, besides the general remark that it lacks 'organization' and 'coordination' and shows 'needless repetition' and 'redundancy' (p. 141), culminates in an implicit denunciation of almost all the hypotheses concerning the early acquisition of languages developed by Penfield, that is, the very essence on which the whole book's fame (at least among educators) rests:

> The book also contains an 'epilogue' by Penfield on the desirability of teaching additional languages at an early age, his argument being based on neurophysiological data. Here, I fear, he falls into a trap usually reserved for physiological psychologists. It is debatable whether there is at present any purely physiological evidence that learning can take place at all, let alone that it is better at one time of life than another. The only evidence we have that children learn in a different way from adults is obtained by observing people learn. Nobody would challenge the behavioural observation that young children learn to *speak* (and to play instruments and games, motor skills of every variety) in a way which can rarely if ever be equalled later in life. But properly controlled research is needed to substantiate the claim that adults find it more difficult to acquire a working knowledge of a second language. (p. 142)
>
> Nevertheless, in spite of the book's misleading analogies, its oversimplified neurophysiology, and its nursery-book style, it may still find some use because it presents for the first time a really elementary version of current ideas in behaviour theory. (p. 143)

What else then does this review result in as far as its underlying theory of language acquisition is concerned? That *Speech and Brain Mechanisms* lacks psychologically valid empirical evidence, that it depends on simplified mental folk-models and that Penfield's hypotheses are nothing more than elementary versions of folk-wisdom, or, as Lenneberg will say, that it contains nothing new on the subject.

It is Hebb then whose ideas have had much deeper influence on the modelling of language processing in the neurosciences and the psychology of language. Some people even claim that his work anticipates — or at least foreshadows — the notion of neural network representation of language. And it is most likely not an accident that Penfield's work before 1944, the year of the first appearance of *The Organization of Behaviour*, is hardly mentioned in Hebb's book. The same is true of Hebb's famous *Textbook of Psychology*, first published in 1958 and translated into various languages — the third edition in 1972 lists eight languages; the chapter on thought and language does not even notice Penfield!

Appendix 3.6

A second important review of *Speech and Brain Mechanisms* is the one by Eric Lenneberg. It was first published in *Language* 36, 97–112 in 1960, and reprinted in R.C. Oldfield and J.C. Marshall (eds) (1968) *Language: Selected Readings* (pp. 333–52), Harmondsworth: Penguin.

This review is a critical account of the state of aphasiology of that time and Penfield's contribution in the light of Lenneberg's own conceptualisations. In view of Lenneberg's own expertise on the topic of the age factor dealt with in the present volume — mainly represented in his seminal work *The Biological Foundations of Language* — this review of the Penfield & Roberts book deserves particular interest. Lenneberg, to be sure, quite in contrast to Penfield, was interested in all of the scientific domains that might touch on the study of the mind and brain, and he carefully prepared himself in each of the pertinent disciplines. Beginning with his MA degree in linguistics from the University of Chicago in 1951, he went on to complete his doctoral studies in both linguistics and psychology at Harvard in 1955. This was followed by three years of postdoctoral specialisation at Harvard Medical School in both neurology and children's developmental disorders. This preparation and additional experience at the Children's Hospital Medical Center in Boston led directly to his now classic monograph on the neuropsychology of language, *The Biological Foundations of Language*, which was published in 1967 (Rieber, 1976: vii). That is to say, Lenneberg's career comprises neurology and linguistics, in other words, two different areas of research and methodologies and, as such, two different levels of describing children's second language acquisition. Again, I should like to restrict myself to discussing the linguistically relevant passages of Lenneberg's review.

> Penfield and Roberts touch on a number of important issues which have recently caused a good deal of discussion in the neurological

> sciences. There is, for instance, the question whether various parts of the brain can and do take over functions normally carried out by other parts. The authors do not take a clear position on this question, which is of paramount importance for our understanding of the neurophysiological nature of language learning. Throughout the book there are statements which would indicate that they firmly believe that taking over is possible and occurs often...yet many of the facts that cast doubt over this concept are also mentioned in the book, though not in connexion with the problem of *taking over.* (reprint, p. 345f.)
>
> The uncertainty concerns the correctness of the phrase 'taking over'. Many neurophysiologists and anatomists doubt that the Central Nervous System has the plasticity which is implied by the notion of taking over. (reprint, p. 346)
>
> There is cogent experimental and clinical-pathological evidence against plasticity; and also from a logical and theoretical standpoint the position becomes untenable. (reprint, p. 346)

Needless to say, these statements definitely contradict Penfield's Plasticity Hypothesis (cf. Appendix 3.2) and may be understood as an implicit criticism of his theory of second language acquisition as well.

> Penfield himself subscribes to the view that there is a physiological facilitation for language acquisition in childhood which disappears in adult life. In fact, the last chapter of the present book [*Speech and Brain Mechanisms*] elaborates this point in great detail, and ends with a plea to educators [*sic*!] to teach foreign languages from the first grade on...
>
> The proponents of the 'taking-over' notion are logically in a...difficult situation. How can the 'mechanism of speech' [please note that this is a critical citation!] be forced from one region of the brain to another? We do not know what *will, consciousness, or purpose* is physiologically or anatomically. Yet we do know that they are all intimately related to neurones and their supportive cells within the brain case. If these cells and their interaction are irreversibly damaged, these mysterious phantasmagorias must be affected as well. There is nothing with a will of its own outside the brain that can decide or will that such and such a part of the brain ought to change its activity to serve this or that purpose.
>
> I have similar difficulties in understanding the authors' conception of their so-called interpretive cortex. ...Undoubtedly, the authors are using metaphorical language, and this is the reason why the reading of these passages conjures up visions of a little man in the brain throwing switches, making decisions, filing records, and interpreting

> sensations. It is clear that the problem of brain mechanisms tends to be obscured through the use of this stylistic device. (reprint, pp. 348f.)

There can be no doubt that Lenneberg must be fully aware of the metaphorical character of scientific language, so what he wants to say is that the folk wisdom type of metaphors in Penfield & Roberts, such as the blend of levels of categorisation and description, is obsolete, which, of course, for Lenneberg amounts to a serious criticism of the underlying theory of language acquisition.

> ...the plea for teaching foreign languages at an early age cannot fail to have a beneficial effect on school teachers [not, to be sure, on researchers investigating or modelling second language acquisition], even though it contains nothing new on the subject. (reprint, p. 350)

'Nothing new on the subject' refers to the lack of empirical evidence and the simple reliance on folk models.

> As a whole the book lacks unity. It is actually not a systematic treatment of the subject of speech and brain mechanisms. We might have hoped that all pertinent facts have been culled from the literature to be presented in a new light, so that much of the confusing information might fall into place; or perhaps that a certain empirical research project had been described and then discussed in all of its implications for a general theory. The book falls short of these expectations. There are a few topics that are dealt with in great detail...while others are only mentioned incidentally. In the latter category is for instance the actual nature of the speech disturbances. This is precisely the area that would particularly interest linguists, and where their skills in language analysis might produce important clinical and theoretical discoveries. But the book makes only a few superficial statements about the phonological derangements of aphasic or electrically stimulated patients, and there is no mention whatever that morphology or syntax either were or were not affected in the utterances of their patients. (reprint, pp. 350f.)

The book (and especially the final chapter, as we would add) neither implicitly nor explicitly proposes nor presupposes a linguistically relevant theory of first and second language production, perception or acquisition as such which might cover, or at least anticipate, the full range of the complexity of language processing.

One might, of course, argue that Penfield as a neurologist and neurosurgeon, unlike Lenneberg without linguistic training, was not aware and simply could not be aware of the dramatic research efforts and discussions dealing with language acquisition in the fifties and sixties.

Lenneberg's organisation of the 17th International Congress of Psychology, which took place in Washington in 1963 and resulted in the famous volume *New Directions in the Study of Language* (1964), represents a characteristic example of this development in a new light. *Speech and Brain Mechanisms* is not even listed in the reference list — despite the fact that the proceedings in question were published not less than ten years after Penfield's Boston lecture and about four years after the Penfield & Roberts volume. However valid this argument may be, it does not rebut the important point we are trying to make that in spite of the obvious fact that Penfield's book is '*not* a systematic treatment of the subject of speech and brain mechanisms' and that it does *not* describe 'a certain empirical research project and then discuss' it 'in all its implications for a general theory'. The point is that it really does make 'only a few superficial statements' concerning linguistic phenomena of (first and second) language acquisition and nevertheless has had, strangely enough, a long and deeply influential impact on language pedagogy.

References

DARDEN, L. 1991, *Theory Change in Science: Strategies from Mendelian Genetics*. New York: Oxford University Press.

FILLMORE, L.W. 1976, The second time around: Cognitive and social strategies in second language acquisition. PhD thesis, Stanford University. Ann Arbor, MI: University Microfilm International.

HEBB, D.O. 1949, *The Organization of Behaviour: A Neurophysiological Theory*. New York: Wiley.

— 1972, *Textbook of Psychology* (3rd edn). Philadelphia: Saunders.

JACOBS, B. and SCHUMANN, J. 1992, Language acquisition and the neurosciences: Towards a more integrative perspective. *Applied Linguistics* 13, 282–99.

KLEIN, W. 1990, A theory of language acquisition is not so easy. *Studies in Second Language Acquisition* 12, 219–31.

LAMBERT, W.E. 1990, Persistent issues in bilingualism. In B. HARLEY, P. ALLEN, J. CUMMINS and M. SWAIN (eds) *The Development of Second Language Proficiency* (pp. 201–20). Cambridge: Cambridge University Press.

LENNEBERG, E.H. 1960, Review of *Speech and Brain Mechanisms* by W. Penfield and L. Roberts. *Language* 36, 97–112. Reprinted in R.C. OLDFIELD and J.C. MARSHALL (eds) 1968, *Language: Selected Readings* (pp. 333–52). Harmondsworth: Penguin.

— (ed.) 1964a, *New Directions in the Study of Language*. Cambridge, MA: MIT Press.

— 1964b, A biological perspective of language. In LENNEBERG (ed.) (pp. 65–88).

— 1967, *The Biological Foundations of Language*. New York: Wiley.

MILNER, P.M. 1960, Review of *Speech and Brain Mechanisms* by W. Penfield and L. Roberts and *Thought and Action* by R.K. Overton. *Canadian Journal of Psychology* 14, 140–3.

— 1970, *Physiological Psychology*. London: Holt, Rinehart and Winston.

— 1993, The mind and Donald O. Hebb. *Scientific American* 268, 124–9.

PENFIELD, W. 1953, A consideration of the neurophysiological mechanisms of speech and some educational consequences. *Proceedings of the American Academy of Arts and Science* 82 (5), 201–13.

— 1965, Conditioning the uncommitted cortex for language learning. *Brain* 88, 787–98.

PENFIELD, W. and ROBERTS, L. 1959, *Speech and Brain Mechanisms*. Princeton, NJ: Princeton University Press.

PETERS, A.M. 1983, *The Units of Language Acquisition*. Cambridge: Cambridge University Press.

RIEBER, R.W. (ed.) 1976, *The Neuropsychology of Language: Essays in Honor of Eric Lenneberg*. New York: Plenum Press.

SIMON, H.A. (ed.) 1979, *Models of Thought*. New Haven and London: Yale University Press.

SINGLETON D. 1989, *Language Acquisition: The Age Factor*. Clevedon: Multilingual Matters.

STERN, H.H. 1967, *Foreign Languages in Primary Education: The Teaching of Foreign or Second Languages to Younger Children*. London: Oxford University Press.

— 1983, *Fundamental Concepts of Language Teaching*. Oxford: Oxford University Press.

WITELSON, S.F. 1987, Neurobiological aspects of language in children. *Child Development* 58, 653–88.

4 Evaluating the Need for Input Enhancement in Post-Critical Period Language Acquisition

GEORGETTE IOUP

There appear to be two features which regularly differentiate child and adult language acquisition. The first is ultimate attainment: children succeed in becoming *bona fide* native speakers, adults by and large don't. The second relates to what has been referred to as input enhancement — explicit structural information given to the learner (Sharwood Smith, 1991). Children learn their native language (L1) without any explicit information on its formal properties. Adult learning (L2), on the other hand, is typically accompanied by some degree of formal instruction and error correction. It is not completely understood how children are able to acquire a language without feedback on its formal properties nor why adults don't succeed with it. Therefore, the characteristics which distinguish child and adult language acquisition create an enigma for language researchers: children who don't receive explicit structural information attain native competence; adults who have access to abundant input enhancement typically don't. To begin to understand why this is so, it is necessary to learn more about the nature of input enhancement and its role in post-critical period language acquisition.

Input Processing in Children

Research studies have shown that children receive little explicit information about the structure of the language they are learning and that any they do receive has minimal effect on the form of the emerging grammar (Brown & Hanlon, 1970; Demetras, Post & Snow, 1986; Hirsh-Pasek, Treiman & Schneiderman, 1984). To build their grammars children rely only on information provided by the sentences in the input they are exposed to which indicate what constitutes a possible sentence. The primary linguistic data (PLD) which supply this information are referred to as positive evidence. Children do not build their grammars using corrective information when they have improperly formulated rules. Feedback of this sort which informs the learner of what is not possible in the language is referred to as negative evidence. Nor do they receive explicit information from those they interact with on such crucial matters as what constitutes a word, what makes something a subject or object, what determines the parts of speech and their various functions, or what defines the inflectional categories. Figuring out this crucial information comprises a fundamental first step before the syntactic rules of the language can emerge. And the child must determine this basic information without explicit help from other speakers. The daunting task of getting started in the language acquisition endeavour is what Pinker (1987) refers to as the bootstrapping problem.

To explain how child language acquisition can proceed using only the positive evidence provided by primary linguistic data, learnability theory assumes that children make use of internal mechanisms which provide constraints on incorrect rule formation. The principal internal mechanism is Universal Grammar (UG), the innate cognitive structure specific to language (Chomsky, 1981). UG contains information which constrains the hypotheses the child initially entertains concerning the possible syntactic and semantic form of a sentence. For example, UG principles prohibit the extraction of a noun phrase embedded within another noun phrase to form a *wh*-question. This principle prevents questioning the italicised word in (1a) to form the ungrammatical sentence given in (1b).

(1a) I heard the news that you called *someone.*

(1b) * Who did you hear the news that I called?

As a result of the constraints of UG, most ungrammatical sentences are never considered by the child.

But not all rules in a language are those constrained by universal principles. There are generalisations in all domains of grammar which are specific to each language and which children learning that language must infer from the input data they receive. When a language-specific rule is hypothesised incorrectly, the child learner cannot rely on explicit negative evidence to reveal that this rule is unacceptable and that it must be altered in some particular way. First language learners must determine by themselves when a rule has been formulated incorrectly and how it needs to be restructured. But this is not a simple matter.

If the rule is too narrow in that it applies to only a subset of the sentences the rule generates in the adult grammar, the child can revise the rule when he or she notices the additional data in the input. But if the hypothesised rule is too broad in that it generates a greater range of structures than the analogous rule in the adult grammar, the child cannot revise it on the basis of positive evidence provided by the input. The child never assumes that he or she has encountered all possible sentences generated by any rule. Therefore, the lack of confirming evidence in the input for a deviant sentence permitted by one of the child's hypotheses will not be grounds for revising the hypothesis.

To enable the child to restructure a rule that overgenerates, mechanisms have been proposed which rely on some form of *pre-emption*: one rule analysis is abandoned for another that fits the data better. Theories explaining restructuring through pre-emption assume that children learning their first language resist having more than one form for the same meaning and that the most frequently occurring form will pre-empt the others. These theories postulate that an overgenerating rule is restructured once the child encounters consistent evidence in the input for a grammatical alternative expressing the same meaning. Among the pre-emption explanations that have been developed in first language acquisition are the uniqueness principle (Pinker, 1984), the principle of contrast (Clark, 1987) and the competition model (MacWhinney, 1987).

Children, therefore, revise their grammars as hitherto unnoticed input data become salient to their innate learning mechanism. This restructuring is achieved without conscious attention to the formal properties of the input. Although their primary aim is to communicate, at a subconscious level children are driven by a need to obtain a match between the output generated by their rule system and the input they perceive. The goal of the innate language acquisition mechanism is to develop an optimal rule system for the target language, one that accounts for the data in the simplest way (White, 1981). Thus, the subconscious restructuring will continue until the competence grammar can optimally account for all the input data.

The lack of conscious attention to form appears to be a characteristic of all child language learning whether the child is learning a first or second language. For example, Wong-Fillmore (1979) detailed the language acquisition experience of five children acquiring English as their second language during the course of one year. She found that the primary goal of all the children was acceptance by their native-speaking peers and language was perceived of only as a tool to enable them to interact socially. Therefore, they paid little attention to the formal properties of the L2.

Nevertheless, their grammars developed normally as they progressed towards native fluency. Only one of the children had any concern for grammatical accuracy and this child made the least progress.

Input Processing in Adults

Adults, in contrast, seem to require some degree of conscious awareness of the language structure when they approach language learning. They do not subconsciously restructure every rule which incorrectly generates the target norm. Therefore, adults typically arrive at a final-state grammar which is replete with non-native constructions. Schmidt (1983), after describing the arrested language development of an adult who had access to abundant primary linguistic data but appeared to be unconcerned with the formal properties of the input, concluded that 'adults seem to have lost the still mysterious ability of children to acquire the grammatical forms of language while apparently not paying attention to them' (p. 172). Schmidt & Frota (1986) maintain that unless an adult *consciously* notices a discrepancy between the form of a structure in the input and the non-target version of it produced by his or her rule system, the non-native construction will resist restructuring and will eventually become a fossilised form. Support for this position, referred to as the 'notice the gap' hypothesis (p. 311), derives from data on Schmidt's own language learning experience in the form of diaries and tape-recorded interactions with native speakers. The authors note that only those constructions in the input that had been noted consciously in Schmidt's diary were subsequently incorporated into his grammar.

A need for conscious awareness of form suggests that some type of input enhancement is necessary for adult language learning. There are several ways that the input to the learner might be enhanced. Explicit information can be provided to the learner on how the language is structured, a form of positive input enhancement. This information may inform the learner of the shape of particular rules, the nature of inflectional paradigms, the identification of categories and functions, etc. Another type of positive input enhancement is a saliency device (Sharwood Smith, 1991). Saliency may come from the classroom teacher or the textbook where particular forms are in some way highlighted to make them more noticeable. Saliency may also be inwardly driven by the learner as he or she makes a conscious attempt to notice particular constructions in the input (as in the 'notice the gap' hypothesis discussed above).

Another type of input enhancement is negative input enhancement consisting of any information the learner receives on what is not possible in the language (i.e. negative evidence). Normally, it is some form of metalinguistic information that an utterance the learner produced was in some fashion deviant or unacceptable. However, Schachter (1986) noted that negative evidence may be a subtle clue such as a clarification request or a look of confusion on the part of the hearer. This type of feedback constitutes indirect negative input enhancement in that it does not provide the learner with information on the exact nature of the error.

Is Input Enhancement Necessary for Adult L2?

There is considerable debate among researchers as to whether input enhancement is requisite or even useful in adult language learning. The debate came to prominence with Krashen who adamantly adheres to a separation between a learned grammar and an acquired grammar. The former consists of explicit knowledge of the language which was gotten through conscious means. According to Krashen, this knowledge will only become part of a metalinguistic system that in no way influences the shape of the acquired grammar, the subconscious linguistic system responsible for producing natural speech. Therefore, information about the language obtained through input enhancement will not contribute to a reorganisation of the underlying L2 competence. Only unenhanced positive evidence in the form of primary linguistic data — the same input which drives child language acquisition — is able to build the acquired grammar. This reasoning is behind the acquisition/learning distinction central to Krashen's Monitor Theory (see Krashen, 1980, 1981).

Many researchers take issue with Krashen's position. Some argue that there is no evidence that enhanced knowledge is unavailable to the underlying grammar and that, therefore, Krashen's claims lack support. Instead, they note, evidence suggests that enhanced input aids the development of L2 grammatical competence (Bialystok, 1981; McLaughlin, 1978; Rutherford, 1988; Sharwood Smith, 1981). Others engage in research demonstrating the contributions of form-focused instruction to the advancement of L2 proficiency. A number of studies have shown short-term gains on particular constructions in the group receiving the focus-on-form treatments (Day & Shapson, 1991; Doughty, 1991; Eckmann, Bell & Nelson, 1988; Gass, 1982; Harley, 1989; Pienemann, 1984; White, Spada, Lightbown & Ranta, 1991).

There are not many studies, however, which examine the long term benefits from form-focused instruction. The findings from the studies which have been done are more suggestive than conclusive. Pavesi (1986) compared the acquisition of English relative clause structures by naturalistic and instructed learners who had on average four to six years' experience with the target language. The instructed group, though they had less exposure to the target language, produced a greater variety of relative clause types including the more difficult, linguistically marked constructions. With few exceptions these were absent from the naturalistic learners' output. However, since the two groups were not equivalent with respect to socioeconomic background and level of education, her results may not be solely the result of differences in formal training.

Higgs & Clifford (1982) proposed that adult naturalistic learners could become fluent but not grammatically accurate in a second language. They based this conclusion on data from students who enrol in language classes at the Foreign Service Institute (FSI). According to their research, those students in the programme who had already gained some degree of L2 fluency through informal learning environments without experiencing focus-on-form instruction never progressed beyond a 2+ ranking (out of a possible 5) on the FSI scale of proficiency. The authors found that their inability to progress to a higher level was due mainly to a lack of progress in the grammatical domain. Van Patten (1988), in responding to their claims, noted that these conclusions were based on personal observation rather than empirical studies.

Therefore, is there evidence that the L2 learner requires conscious awareness of specific constructions in order to formulate hypotheses to generate them? The debate has been taken up with renewed vigour as researchers now question whether aspects of the L2 which derive from Universal Grammar can be affected when augmented with enhanced input. The issue is whether a L2 learner who has incorrectly assumed an L1 setting for a parameter that has a different value in the L2 can correctly reset the parameter without explicit, externally generated input — both positive and negative.

Schwartz (1986, 1993), building on Fodor's modularity of mind theory, argues that only primary linguistic data — i.e. positive unenhanced input — are the type of information that can be utilised by the language acquisition module in both first and second language acquisition. Explicit input only assists the development of learned linguistic knowledge, which then produces learned linguistic behaviour. It does not contribute to the growth and reorganisation of the internal competence grammar which is the only system able to produce natural L2 speech. Schwartz's position is similar to that of Krashen. Schwartz does add, however, that her arguments are valid only for the acquisition of syntactic aspects of the language. Morphological and lexical information is likely to be acquired as learned linguistic knowledge, since these domains require incremental learning of individual pieces of information. Furthermore, in contrast to Krashen's theory, this type of learned linguistic knowledge can generate speech, which Schwartz refers to as learned linguistic behaviour. In her view this learned knowledge does not integrate into the competence grammar.

To determine whether form-focused instruction and corrective feedback could, in fact, aid in resetting an incorrectly set parameter, White (1991) examined the verb movement parameter in French speakers learning English. She observed that French learners of English assume a parameter setting for verb movement in their L2 that is only valid for the L1. Subjects selected for the study were divided into two groups, one of which received intensive form-focused instruction on the relevant construction. The control group engaged in normal communicative language learning activities which contained no explicit information pertaining to the parameter. Results showed that on both immediate and delayed post-testing, only the group receiving enhanced input gave indication of resetting the parameter. However, in follow-up testing one year later, the experimental group did not retain the new setting, indicating that, in this case, the form-focused instruction produced no lasting effect.

Commenting on the White (1991) study, Trahey & White (1993) noted that in retrospect, the control group seldom encountered the relevant structures in the naturalistic input they received. Therefore, no conclusions could be drawn from the results on the possibility of resetting a L2 parameter with only unenhanced input. In the 1993 study, they specifically set out to study whether the L1 setting would be pre-empted when the learner was exposed to abundant PLD consistent only with the L2 setting. French ESL learners were 'flooded' with naturalistic L2 input replete with constructions requiring a resetting of the verb movement parameter. Results showed that the unenhanced positive evidence did not bring about a pre-emption of the L1 parameter setting. Nevertheless, the authors could not conclude that their findings demonstrated the inability of PLD by itself to trigger the resetting a parameter in L2 acquisition. The outcome could have resulted from a number of secondary factors including the possibility that the duration of the treatment period was not long enough to give sufficient exposure to the target structures, or that the time required to reset a parameter is longer than the interval between the treatment and the final testing. Thus, to this point no empirical studies give conclusive evidence of limitations on PLD or the value of enhanced input to trigger restructuring in post critical period language acquisition.

Maturational Changes Affecting Language Learning

Why would input enhancement be necessary for adult language learning? It has been hypothesised that as the human matures, changes occur in neurocognitive organisation which lead to diminished language learning capacity. Explanations of the changes which occur take several forms. There are those who maintain that older learners no longer have access to the innate language acquisition mechanism and therefore, approach language learning using general learning principles (Bley-Vroman, 1990; Clahsen 1990; Schachter, 1989). Others argue that the innate mechanism still operates fully, but is impeded by other cognitive factors. Felix (1985) posits that in the adult, problem solving cognitive structures compete with the language-specific structures in analysing the L2 input data to which they are applied inappropriately. Flynn (1989) and White (1989, 1992) attribute the difficulties of the older learner to the influence of the language already acquired: the parameter settings of the first language are adopted into the new language. Each of the above explanations assumes the adult will require explicit instruction and negative evidence to formulate correctly the rules of the L2 grammar.

The apparent inability of adults to acquire native competence from PLD alone has led researchers to postulate a critical period for language acquisition terminating at about the onset of puberty (Penfield & Roberts, 1959; Lenneberg, 1967). There is debate as to whether the hypothesised critical period pertains solely to the acquisition of the first language or applies to the acquisition of both the first and subsequent languages. On the former view, once a primary language is acquired before puberty, there is no cognitive barrier to the acquisition of subsequent languages after puberty. On the latter view, after a certain age, no language learning can achieve native-like standards. To support the second position are several experimental studies which demonstrate that L2 learners with long-term residence have retained non-native features in their grammars (Johnson & Newport, 1989; Oyama, 1976; Patkowski, 1980), even those who on the surface appear native-like (Coppieters, 1987; Scarcella, 1983)[1].

A number of studies, however, discuss atypical adult language learners who appear to have attained native-like proficiency in their second language (Birdsong, 1992; Novoa, Fein & Obler, 1989; Schneiderman & Desmarais, 1988b; Sorace, 1993; White & Genesee 1993)[2]. These learners are said to have talent or aptitude for learning language resulting from special neurocognitive abilities (Obler, 1989; Schneiderman & Desmarais, 1988a). While the learners in these studies are said to approach native-speaker levels of proficiency, the studies indicate that they have experienced form-focused instruction. Thus these learners, though successful, appear to take a different path to acquisition than child learners.

What is it that form-focused instruction provides the language learner? First, the classroom breaks down the code at the initial stages to accomplish the bootstrapping of L1 acquisition (Pinker, 1987). Second, it presents the structures of the language in a sequentially organised fashion, according to some predetermined order of difficulty. Next it provides ready-made rule hypotheses about these structures. Finally, it brings to the learner's awareness any deviations from the target norm. These are challenges the child learner and the naturalistic adult learner must overcome alone.

Yet, in spite of the adult's apparent need for externally generated input enhancement, there are reports of adult L2 learners who are able to achieve near-native levels of proficiency without it. They seem to be able to acquire the language using internally generated input enhancement supplemented with only haphazard, nonsystematic negative feedback. Several questions arise concerning these learners. First, have they in fact acquired an underlying competence which mirrors the native speaker's? Second, is their linguistic development similar to that of instructed learners who have reached an equivalent level of proficiency? Restated in terms of the issues raised earlier in this paper, does input enhancement lead to differences in ultimate attainment? Finally, how relevant is conscious awareness of structure to the language learning experience?

Comparing the Ultimate Attainment of Two Near-Native Speakers

To shed light on these questions, this paper reports on a study which compares the mental grammars of two near-native speakers of Egyptian Arabic (EA), one instructed and one naturalistic. Both are educated native speakers of English who have married Egyptians and are long-term residents of Cairo. The study first assesses their proficiency through an evaluation of their linguistic performance. It then investigates their mental grammars by examining their intuitions on remote constructions in EA related to Universal Grammar, language particular syntax, and anaphoric interpretation.

Subjects

The first subject in the study is Julie, an untutored learner. She has never had formal instruction in Arabic and, therefore, can neither read nor write the language. Julie emigrated to Cairo from Britain at the age of 21 when she married an Egyptian. Nine days after her arrival her husband was unexpectedly called to military service and she was left with non-English-speaking relatives for 45 days. Since there was no one to assist her in English, she relied on context and gesture to interpret utterances and express meaning. Thus, at this initial stage her language acquisition situation resembled the environment for child L1 acquisition. After her husband's return from the military, she continued to receive abundant EA input on a daily basis. One year after her arrival Julie took a position as an English teacher in an Egyptian school where she conversed with monolingual colleagues in Arabic. Beginning with her third year of stay, Arabic became the home language because at this point her fluency was sufficiently developed to permit her to converse comfortably in the L2. At the time of the study she had lived in Egypt for 26 years and was working as an ESL teacher/trainer at the university level.

In terms of the process of her acquisition, Julie recalls the following points. To facilitate communication during her early total immersion, she kept a copybook in which she wrote what she observed concerning the language. At first her notations were unanalysed wholes with attempts at guessing meanings. Soon she began to keep separate pages for nouns, verbs, and adjectives. Lexical meaning was the main priority, but some elements of inflectional morphology were noted, especially changes involving gender, number, and person. The copybook was kept for three to four months.

Explicit feedback was received when her errors hampered communication. Feedback usually took the form of corrected or expanded repetitions. She frequently made mental or written note of the point of the correction. Effective communication was her only goal; therefore, she was not concerned with grammatical structure except as a means to achieve this end. By the end of six months, she was communicating rather well. After two and one half years she was able to pass as a native speaker[3].

With respect to the acquisition of the different domains of the grammar, she reports that phonology was no problem, even initially, as she has a talent for mimicking accents. Even the difficult pharyngeal and uvular consonants were easily perceived and reproduced. As to her acquisition of morphological structure, Julie consciously noted the inflections and clitics pertaining to gender, number, and person. She doesn't recall being aware of the phonotactic adjustments which accompany morphophonemic alternations. The complex rules of syntax were also acquired without conscious attention to form. Even tense distinctions were not consciously noted. Julie reports that she is not sure how she mastered syntactic aspects of the grammar, but somehow they just came. Nevertheless, Julie did respond to negative input which most likely contained feedback on selected syntactic structures. On the basis of her self-report, Julie's grammatical acquisition appears to resemble Schwartz's (1993) predictions. She employed the 'notice the gap' strategy more consistently with morphology and the lexicon then with syntax or the subtleties of phonology.

The instructed subject selected for comparison is Laura. She was reported to have achieved a native-like level of proficiency in EA through extensive formal instruction. Laura is an American who is married to an Egyptian and is living in Cairo. She had many years of formal instruction in standard Arabic before beginning the study of EA. She commenced the study of standard Arabic during her senior year as an undergraduate, continuing it in France for two years after graduation. After a one-year sojourn in Morocco, where she taught English and acquired the rudiments of Moroccan Arabic, she returned to the US to obtain a master's degree in modern standard Arabic. She then commenced a PhD in the language, working at the same time as an Arabic teaching assistant. Because she could read but not converse in Arabic, she interrupted her doctoral programme to study the spoken Egyptian dialect at the American University in Cairo. She remained in Cairo after her programme ended, married an Egyptian, and became a teacher of standard Arabic. At the time of the study Laura had lived in Egypt for ten years and was teaching modern standard Arabic as a foreign language at the university level.

Thus, Laura's first exposure to both the written and spoken dialects was in the classroom as an adult, and she studied both varieties extensively. Her L2 experience consisted of the typical analytic approach to formal instruction, enriched by communicative classroom exercises and daily-life interactions in the second language environment. In terms of communicative style, Laura is a careful speaker. She reports that she often consciously attempts to avoid grammatical errors when she produces EA utterances. She is reflective as she speaks and listens, frequently noticing minor errors in native-speaker speech. As an Arabic language teacher, she is constantly interacting with the formal properties of the language.

Proficiency evaluation

To determine whether the two subjects had achieved similar levels of proficiency, three procedures were employed to elicit performance data: a speech production task, an accent identification task and a translation task.

Speech Production

The first procedure evaluated the two subjects' spoken language to determine if, in fact, they would be considered native speakers by Egyptian judges. Spontaneous speech was elicited by asking subjects to detail their favourite recipe on tape. Five other female speakers also performed the task. Three were educated native speakers of the Cairene dialect of Arabic; the other two were very fluent non-native speakers who were long time residents of Cairo, but who nevertheless retained noticeable non-native features in their speech. Judges for the task were 13 teachers of Arabic as a foreign language. They were asked to decide whether or not each speaker was a native Egyptian and to state their reasons for any negative judgments given. The goal was to determine whether the two subjects would be grouped with the native or non-native speakers.

All judges correctly categorised the three native-speaking and the two non-native-speaking distractors (other than Julie and Laura) as native and non-native, respectively. Julie and Laura were rated as native speakers by eight of the 13 judges (62%). Only native speakers particularly sensitive to phonetic discrimination were able to notice non-native qualities in their speech[4].

Accent Identification

The second area of performance testing concerned the two subjects' ability to discriminate among regional accents of EA, a skill said to reflect native-like competence (Scovel, 1981). They were asked to decide whether or not an accent was the Cairene variety of EA. The phonological properties which distinguish regional dialects in Egypt are very subtle. To make the task more difficult, one of the three speakers to be evaluated had moved to Cairo from another part of the country so that her dialect was not pure Cairene, but a blend. Speaker 1 had a lower Egyptian accent, Speaker 2 a Cairene accent, and Speaker 3 a modified Cairene accent. Eleven judges from the previous procedure served as NS controls.

Not all of the native speaking judges were able to detect the non-Cairene features in Speaker 3. Only five of the 11 identified her correctly. On this task Julie and Laura do not perform identically. Julie is closer to the native responses. Laura stated that she could detect no difference among the three accents in that they all sounded Cairene. Julie, on the other hand, performs like the majority of the native speakers who were able to identify Speaker 1 correctly as non-Cairene, but did not hear the subtle non-Cairene cues in Speaker 3.

Translation

The third performance measure assessed the subjects' ability to translate selected constructs into Arabic. The sentences used each contained a rule governed contrast related to relative clauses, yes/no questions, *wh*-questions, and conjoined NPs. All of the contrasts centred on rules that are very specialised to EA and are not directly translatable from English. Sentence (1) below is a sample item from the translation procedure together with a typical EA translation:

(1) Which book was it that Mona bought?
anhi kitaab illi mona ishtarit-u
which book that mona bought-it

Eleven native speakers were also evaluated for comparison. None of them served as judges in the previous two procedures. All of them were university graduates, five of them specialising in languages, six in sciences. All were fluent in English, ensuring that they could follow directions and perform the translation task competently.

The 11 native and two near-native test-takers were given a list of 12 English sentences to translate and record onto tape. They were instructed to give a spontaneous translation with minimal preplanning. The responses of Julie and Laura were scored first on their accuracy with respect to the contrasts tested, then on overall structure. Responses were considered correct if they matched a translation given by at least one native speaker for that item. In every respect Julie and Laura gave virtually flawless responses. They scored perfectly on the grammatical contrasts tested. The complexities of morphology were produced with 100% accuracy. There was little that was not native-like elsewhere.

However, both Julie and Laura on one occasion used the same preposition in a non-native fashion, seemingly unaware of its obligatory deletion in certain contexts. It should be noted that on the grammatical judgment task to be described next, they both accepted as grammatical a sentence where this preposition was correctly deleted.

In addition, Julie utilised the yes/no question particle incorrectly on one occasion when translating a relative clause with an emphatic subject, as illustrated in sentence (2) below.

(2) Nadia is the one that Ahmad saw.
NS form: *nadya heyya illi ahmad shaf-ha*
nadia she that aḥmad saw-her
Julie: *heyya nadya illi aḥmad shaf-ha*
Q nadya that ahmad saw-her

The 3rd person singular pronouns *huwwa* (masculine) and *heyya* (feminine), in addition to their normal pronominal usage, can function as emphatic subject markers, in which case they follow the noun, or as optional indicators of yes/no questions, in which case they occur in sentence-initial position. Julie's word order here is that of a question rather than a statement. In her other translation sentences the word order distinction was correctly made for both functions.

From the above three measures it was determined that Julie and Laura have indeed achieved similar levels of proficiency, though each through a different route, justifying further comparison of them.

Assessing their mental grammars

A more interesting concern is whether the two learners have internalised similar rule systems in the L2. Only when this question is settled can one begin to determine the effect of form-focused instruction on the L2 grammar. To assess their underlying knowledge, both syntactic and semantic aspects of the language were examined. The testing instrument consisted of a two-part procedure containing a grammaticality judgment test and a task to measure the interpretation of anaphora. The points tested are subtle, and are typically difficult for L2 learners of EA. They are derived from both principles of Universal Grammar and rules specific to EA. The sentences used in this procedure were drawn from the research of Farghaly (1982) and Osman (1990), and from the author's personal experience with L2 learners of EA. Native-speaking controls for these procedures were the same eleven Egyptians who performed the translation measure. Because Julie cannot read Arabic, all sentences to be evaluated were recorded on tape to be responded to individually.

Grammatical Judgment Task

The first assessment of their mental grammar was a grammaticality judgment task where test-takers were asked to indicate on an answer sheet whether a recorded sentence was grammatical or ungrammatical. The sentences were read at a rapid rate with only a few seconds pause between each. The task included 37 EA sentences representing different syntactic structures. Test items included structures from two domains of syntax: those pertaining to constraints in UG and those that follow from language-particular rules of EA. Before discussing the individual test items, it is necessary to describe certain important properties of EA.

Egyptian Arabic is distinct from standard Arabic and the other colloquial dialects in two important respects, both relating to word order. First, whereas standard Arabic and the other colloquial dialects have relatively free canonical word order, with one of them functioning as the unmarked variant, EA has a fixed word order of SVO. It does not allow deviations from this canonical order except in rare situations, not even for stylistic purposes. The second difference concerns the formation of *wh*-questions. While standard Arabic and the other colloquial dialects form *wh*-questions by fronting the *wh*-phrase, Egyptian Arabic typically forms them by leaving the *wh*-phrase *in-situ*, although adverbial *wh*-phrases can be optionally fronted.

The sentences relating to UG were drawn from the work of Osman (1990). They include violations of the complex NP constraint, the superiority constraint, and the binding principles (cf. Chomsky, 1981). These constraints and principles operate in English also, but in a manner different from Egyptian Arabic as a result of basic differences in the way movement rules operate in the two languages[5].

Sentences relevant to the complex NP constraint are illustrated in (3a) and (3b). Osman (1990) finds sentences like (3b), where fronting the *wh*-phrase violates the UG principle of subjacency, ungrammatical. In contrast, sentences like (3a), where the *wh*-phrase is left *in-situ*, are deemed grammatical. In English, on the other hand, there is no grammatical way to form a question from inside a complex NP — unless one is asking an echo question.

(3a) *fatḥi simi il-axbaar in samiir saafir ma' miin*
fathi heard the-news that samir left with whom

(3b) * *ma' miin fatḥi simi il-axbaar in samiir saafir*
with whom fathi heard the-news that samir left
'With whom did Fathi hear the news that Samir left?'

The superiority condition operates slightly differently in EA and English. In English, when there is a *wh*-phrase in both subject and postverbal position, the postverbal phrase can never be fronted.

(4a) Who left with whom?

(4b) * With whom who left?

In EA a postverbal *wh*-phrase can be fronted if the subject *wh*-phrase has first been shifted to a position following the verb, thereby allowing it to receive government. This is illustrated in the paradigm in (5).

(5a) *miin xarag ma' miin*
who left with whom

(5b) * *ma' miin miin xarag*
with whom who left

(5c) *ma' miin xarag miin*
with whom left who
'Who left with whom?'

The third UG derived construct tested relates to the occurrence of overt proforms (resumptive pronouns) in relative clauses. Osman (1990) notes that proforms, when occurring inside *wh*-constructions, are realised as resumptive pronominal clitics in all positions but subject, which is obligatorily null. This follows from the requirements of the binding theory. An overt resumptive pronoun in the subject position of a relative clause will be locally bound, violating Principle B of the binding theory. Resumptive pronouns filling other positions in the relative clause are not bound locally, and as a result no violation occurs. Only sentences with resumptive pronouns in non-subject position are grammatical and are required in these positions. Sentences (6) and (7) illustrate the contrast.

(6a) *ir-raagil illi ayyaan kallim-ak*
the-man that sick called-you
(6b) * *ir-raagil illi huwwa ayyan kallim-ak*
the-man that he sick called-you
'The man who is sick called you'.
(7a) *ir-raagil illi mona abilt-uh fi-l-maktaba maṣri*
the-man that mona met-him in-the-library Egyptian
(7b) * *ir-raagil illi mona abilt fi-l-maktaba maṣri*
the-man that mona met in-the-library Egyptian
'The man that Mona met in the library is Egyptian'.

English does not allow resumptive pronouns in any position.

The final contrast based on the constraints of UG pertains to the distribution of the question particle which was described earlier. The question particle is limited to matrix clause questions, never occurring in embedded questions, as shown in (8a) and (b).

(8a) *Hiyya mona irfit samiir raaḥ feen*
Q mona knew samir went where
'Did Mona know where Samir went?'
(8b) * *mona irfit huwwa samiir raaḥ feen*
mona knew Q samir went where
'Mona knew where Samir went'.

It is not well understood what principle of UG restricts certain syntactic phenomena to matrix clause positions, but such structures are found in many of the world's languages. Structures restricted to the matrix clause appear to relate in some way to the speaker's disposition toward the utterance. In the present case, the speaker is specifying that the utterance is a question.

The language-particular constructs used on this task involve rules governing definiteness concord, the particulars of relativised structures, and word order possibilities related to conjoined NPs and questions. With respect to definiteness concord, EA adjectives and relative clauses must agree with their heads in definiteness. Typically, English speakers learning Arabic fail to observe this requirement by omitting the definite marker on definite adjectives or by inserting the relative marker, which is definite, on indefinite relative clauses.

There are two other interesting properties concerning relative structures. When a nominal *wh*-phrase is focused in question initial position, the remainder of the sentence takes the form of a relative clause. Thus the complete question consists of only a question word and a relative clause. These are referred to as relativised questions.

(9) *miin illi samiir kallim-u*
who that samir called-him
'Who did Samir call?'

EA also manifests headless relative clauses where a normal definite relative clause can occur without a head or any internal changes.

(10) *illi gaah kallim-ak*
that came called-you
'(The man) who came called you'.

Both of these constructs seem odd to English-speaking learners.

The remaining language-particular items involve word order in conjoined NPs and in questions. Conjoined NPs, where at least one member is a pronominal form, must obey a strict order which is different from that of English. The order is determined by the person and number of the pronoun, and by whether it is joined to another pronoun or to a full NP. Word order in questions was discussed earlier.

The test contained five categories relating to language-particular constructs and four relating to Universal Grammar. A complete list of the grammatical constructs used on this task and examples of each are given in Appendix 4.1.[6] To evaluate the performance of Julie and Laura, we followed Coppieters (1987) in establishing a prototypical native norm corresponding to NS majority opinion on each item. We then determined where Julie and Laura diverged from the prototype. Table 4.1 presents the results on this task.

Table 4.1 NNS divergence[1] from NS grammaticality judgments of language-particular and UG-constrained constructs

	Item No.	*NS Agreement (%) N = 11*	*NS*	*Judgments*	
				Julie	*Laura*
Language-particular constructs					
Definiteness concord	3	100	Yes		
	33	100	Yes		
	36	100	No		
	12	91	Yes		
	19	91	No		Yes
	6	82	No		
	1	82	No		
	14	73	No	Yes	
Relavitised questions	35	100	No		
	17	91	No		
	22	91	No		
	21	73	Yes		
	26	64	No		
Headless relative clauses	9	73	Yes		
	7	55	Yes		
Conjoined NP word order	24	100	Yes		
	8	73	No		Yes
	28	73	No		Yes
	4	73	Yes		
	27	55	Yes		

Table 4.1 indicates the majority NS grammaticality judgment for each test item and where Julie and Laura diverge from the majority response. A considerable range of variation was found in native-speaker responses, with agreement on particular items ranging from 55% to 100%. As on all tasks involving grammaticality judgments, there were several sentences which were rejected by some of the native speakers with no apparent explanation. However, some of the results show where there is indeterminacy in the language and, therefore, genuine disagreement among native speakers. The sentence types involving *wh*-movement fall into this category. Since there was considerable variability in response patterns among

Table 4.1 (*cont.*)

	Item No.	*NS Agreement (%) N = 11*	*NS*	*Judgments*	
				Julie	*Laura*
Language-particular Constructs					
Variable word order in questions	32	100	Yes		
	25	100	Yes	No	
	37	91	Yes	No	No
	18	73			
	2	55			
UG-constrained					
Resumptive proforms in embedded sentences	16	100	Yes		
	10	100	Yes		
	5	100	No		
	13	73	No		
	11	64	No	Yes	Yes
Multiple *wh*-questions	15	91	Yes		
	23	64	No		
	29	64	No		
Distribution of Yes/No question particle	30	100	Yes		
	20	55	No	Yes	
Complex NP constraint	34	73	No		
	31	73	No		Yes

Yes = acceptance of item as grammatical. No = rejection of item as ungrammatical.
1. Only those responses by Julie and Laura which diverge from the majority NS response are indicated

native speakers on sentences involving *wh*-movement, NSs were questioned individually about their degree of certainty on these items. None of the native speakers changed their minds or even hesitated in reaffirming their intuitions.

As can be seen in Table 4.1, the performance of both Julie and Laura was comparable to that of native speakers in the majority of cases. The divergence which did occur was exhibited, for the most part, on sentences with less than 80% native speaker agreement, indicating that at least three native speakers shared their opinion. In general, disagreements consisted of judging ungrammatical sentences as grammatical.

It is interesting to examine the particular items where the two subjects deviated from the NS majority response. Both Julie and Laura accepted an ungrammatical sentence where the adjective did not agree in definiteness with the head, but correctly rejected another of the same type (items 14 and 19). With conjoined NP structures, Laura, but not Julie, accepted all the variants as grammatical, possibly not aware of the restrictions governing the ordering of nouns and pronouns in co-ordinate NPs, where, unlike English, for example, a pronominal form must precede a full NP, and first person pronouns precede those of the second person.

Both Julie and Laura deviated from the NS norm in their assessment of optional word order variations in questions. Native speakers allowed more scrambling possibilities. For example, unlike 91% of the native speakers, they rejected the question shown in 11 with a fronted question word and subject/verb inversion (item 37) as ungrammatical:

(11) *imta saafrit nadya*
when left nadia
'When did Nadia leave?'

Julie, in particular, seemed to reject variable word order in questions, insisting on *in-situ wh*-phrases, the unmarked word order, throughout the test.

In general, both Julie and Laura performed surprisingly well. Of the total of 37 sentences, Julie had divergent judgments on five, Laura on six. Two of Julie's five divergent judgments consisted of rejecting optional variants; the other three were failures to reject sentences the majority judged ungrammatical. Laura rejected one optional variant and accepted as grammatical five sentences judged ungrammatical by the majority. Their deviations occurred on both language-particular and UG-derived constructs.

Our data do not allow us to conclude that the two learners were unable to apply the principles of UG to L2 data since each deviation from a UG-derived constraint was shared by many of the NSs. We can assume, therefore, that both Julie and Laura share intuitions with native speakers on the majority of the syntactic points tested. However, it is important to note that though many native speakers deviated from the norm in their judgments as frequently as Julie and Laura, none exhibited patterns in the same way as the two subjects (for example, on conjoined NP word order, for Laura, or on optional word order in questions, for Julie), but deviated in a more random manner. Additional testing would provide a clearer comparison of the internal organisation of the near-native and native grammars.

The Interpretation of Anaphora

The second task in this part of the study dealt with the interpretation of anaphora, based on Farghaly's (1982) discussion of the disambiguating function of overt subject pronouns in embedded clauses. An example of this function is illustrated in the following pair of sentences.

(12a) *nadya shaafit mona lamma daxalit il-ooda*
nadia saw mona when entered the-room.

(12b) *nadya shaafit mona lamma heyya daxalit il-ooda*
nadia saw mona when she entered the-room
'Nadia saw Mona when (she) entered the room'.

The absence of an overt subject pronoun in (12a) gives rise to a preferred interpretation that assigns the *adjacent* NP (Mona) as the subject of the verb *daxalit*. In contrast, the overt subject pronoun in (12b) indicates disjoint reference with the adjacent NP (Mona), crossing instead to the more *remote* NP (Nadia) as the preferred antecedent.

This task included 18 recorded sentences. Each sentence contained a main clause with one to three lexical NPs coupled with a conjoined or embedded clause manifesting either a null or overt subject pronoun. The sentences represent the different syntactic categories shown in Table 4.2. The test-takers were asked to respond to the question 'Who did X?' where *did X* is the predicate of the embedded clause. This procedure made it possible to determine what reference test-takers were assigning. Answers could be written in either Arabic script, transliteration, or English translation. Table 4.2 gives the results on this task.

Here one can see a difference in the performance of Julie and Laura. Laura interprets reference in the same manner as the NS norm. Julie, on the other hand, made the distinction between overt and empty proforms in co-ordinate and preposed subordinate structures only. When the anaphora occurred inside a relative clause, she did not distinguish between the two. Consistently she assigned adjacent reference to a sentence with an overt subject pronoun in the relative clause.

The sentences containing relative clauses were deliberately complex, so even native speakers found them difficult to process. There was substantially more variability among native speakers in their interpretation of anaphora in relative clauses than in conjoined sentences or with backward pronominalisation. Julie indicated that she had considerable difficulty keeping track of noun phrases in the relative clause structures. It may be that her divergence on these items is due to problems in processing these complex sentences, rather than difficulty in assigning reference. To

Table 4.2 NNS divergence from NS preferred interpretation of anaphora in three syntactic categories

Syntactic category	*Item No.*	*NS Agreement (%)*	*NNS Divergence*	
		N = 11	*Julie*	*Laura*
Conjoined sentence				
Adjacent reference	2	100		
Remote reference	8	100		
Backward prononinalisation				
Adjacent reference	18	91		
Remote reference	16	100		
Relative clause				
Adjacent reference	1	73	Remote	
	3	91		
	5	64		
	7	100		
	10	91		
Remote reference	6	64	Adjacent	
	11	73	Adjacent	
	13	91	Adjacent	
	14	82	Adjacent	
	15	82	Adjacent	

Sentences which received a NS preferred interpretation of adjacent reference contained embedded null subjects. Those which received a preferred interpretation of remote reference contained embedded overt pronominal subjects.
Only NNS divergence from majority NS interpretation of an item is indicated.

ascertain which was the case, one would need to assess her performance on sentences of this type that are less complex. In any case, her performance diverged from that of native speakers.

This task deals with discourse semantics and is the only one which consistently distinguishes Julie from native speakers. It is interesting that Coppieters (1987) also found that his near-native speakers gave more incorrect hypotheses on discourse semantic constructs than on sentence-level syntax. Perhaps additional testing in this area will reveal domains where the grammar of a successful naturalistic learner is incomplete.

Assessing the Effects of Input Enhancement

It appears, however, that these two learners, one tutored and one untutored, have, by and large, achieved similar grammatical competence in EA. There seems to be little that distinguishes a successful learner with formal instruction from one without. The differences noted between Julie and Laura were minor. Julie has better perceptual skills for accent recognition. Laura is unaware of co-ordinate NP word order restrictions which Julie has mastered. Julie is more rigid with regard to optional word order possibilities and has more difficulty with one type of anaphoric reference.

The data presented in this study lead one to hypothesise that for those few L2 learners who are able to achieve a native-like level of proficiency, formal instruction does not result in a markedly different mental grammar. Whatever bootstrapping, sequencing, rule analysis and negative input form-focused instruction provides, successful naturalistic L2 learners are able to do this for themselves. Most certainly, they accomplish this by relying on an internal language acquisition mechanism that is able to provide sufficient internally generated input enhancement. But this alone cannot explain why certain naturalistic learners can achieve native-like proficiency without explicit form-focused instruction, while others can barely get past the rudiments of the grammar. Certainly, the explanation must lie in an understanding of their unique neurocognitive abilities. It has been hypothesised that talented learners possess a neurocognitive organisation that is in some way distinct from that of the average language learner. However, the exact nature of this difference is not well understood (Ioup *et al.*, 1994; Obler, 1989; Schneiderman & Desmarais, 1988a; Smith & Tsimple, 1991).

One might conclude from Julie's success that input enhancement is a not a prerequisite for native-like attainment in adult language learning. But this is not a valid conclusion. Julie provided herself with abundant internally generated input enhancement. As a learner she made a constant effort to become aware of the structural properties of the L2. She compiled organised notes about the language structure as she gained insights. These notes were reviewed and revised as her insights changed. She also welcomed corrective feedback and availed herself of the negative evidence it provided. In contrast, the unsuccessful naturalistic learner described in Schmidt (1983) typically ignored structural information provided to him.

However, it is important to note that the areas of language structure which became salient to Julie were the phonemic contrasts, lexical meaning, the inventory of morphological forms, and the more surface rules of syntax

— the very types of information taught in typical form-focused classrooms. She was not consciously aware of the structural regularities pertaining to the subtle aspects of syntax and morphophonology. Yet, the data show that she has mastered the majority of the rule governed constructs in these domains. The findings from this study would give support both to those who argue for and to those who argue against a place for form-focused instruction. It seems that input enhancement (whether internally or externally generated) is necessary to master those aspects of the language which Schwartz (1993) notes involve the learning of individual constructions, whereas the subtleties that derive from UG and thereby require a clustering of properties, are acquired by an active language acquisition mechanism through experience with PLD. However, contrary to Schwartz's beliefs, both Julie and Laura appear to have integrated their learned linguistic knowledge into their underlying competence grammar.

Acknowledgements

The data reported on in this article were collected in collaboration with three students at the American University in Cairo: Elizabeth Boustagui, Manal El Tigi, and Martha Moselle. The portions of this article detailing the two exceptional language learners appear in greater detail in Ioup *et al.* (1994).

Notes

1. For an extensive review of the literature on the Critical Period Hypothesis and its relevance to second language acquisition, see Long (1990).
2. Selinker (1972) estimates the number of such talented individuals to be about 5% of adult language learners.
3. Corroborating Julie's own memory of this period, Egyptian colleagues of the author who interacted with her in these early years recollect her native-like ability at that point.
4. In the case of Julie, judges did not specify the same words or consonants as indicators of non-nativeness. The reasons for their decisions varied from judge to judge. On the other hand, the assessments of Laura when judged as non-native were more consistent.
5. For a fuller description of the syntactic structure of EA and the manner in which these constraints operate in it, see Ioup *et al.* (1994).
6. The number of test items in a category was a function of the syntactic requirements of the construct. For example, definiteness concord required eight test items: a grammatical and ungrammatical exemplar of both definite and indefinite adjectives and relative clauses.

Appendix 4.1: Examples of Constructs Used on Grammaticality Judgment Task

Language Particular

Definiteness Concord

aabilt ir-raagil il-mashhur
met-I the-man the-famous

* *aabilt ir-raagil mashhur*
met-I the-man famous
'I met the famous man'.

Relativised Questions

miin illi aḥmad aabl-u
who that ahmad met-him

* *miin aḥmad aabl-u*
who ahmad met-him
'Who is it that Ahmad met?'

Headless Relative Clauses

illi bint-u gat muhandes kibiir
that girl-his came engineer great
'(The one) whose daughter came is a great engineer'.

Conjoined NP Word Order

nadya raaḥit ma'aah huwwa wi 'ali in-naadi
nadia went with-him him and ali the-club

* *nadya raaḥit ma' 'ali wi ma'aah in-naadi*
nadia went with ali and with-him the-club
'Nadia went with Ali and him to the club'.

Variable Word Order in Questions

heyya samiira ti'raf mona raaḥit feen
Q samira know mona went where

* *heyya samiira ti'raf feen raaḥit mona*
Q samira know where went mona
'Does Samira know where Mona went?'

UG Constrained

Resumptive Proforms in Embedded Sentences

il-bint di min iṣ-ṣa'b it-taḥakkum fii-ha
the-girl this from the-difficult the-control in-her

**il-bint di min iṣ-ṣa'b it-taḥakkum fii*
the-girl this from the-difficult the-control in
'This girl is difficult to control'.

Multiple wh-Questions

miin xarag ma' miin
who left with who

** ma' miin xarag miin*
with who left who
'Who left with whom?'

Yes/No Question Particle

heyya nadya ti'raf aḥmad gaab il-kutub min-een
Q nadia know ahmad got the-book from-where

** nadya ti'raf huwwa aḥmad gaab il-kutub min-een*
nadia know Q ahmad got the-book from-where
'Does Nadia know where Ahmad got the book from?'

Complex NP Constraint

ma' miin 'ali simi' in mona saafrit
with who ali heard that mona travelled

** ma' miin 'ali simi' il-axbaar in mona saafrit*
with who ali heard the-news that mona travelled
'With whom did Ali hear (the news) that Mona travelled?'

References

BIALYSTOK, E. 1981, Some evidence for the integrity and interaction of two knowledge sources. In R. ANDERSON (ed.) *New Dimensions in Second Language Acquisition Research* (pp. 62–74). Rowley, MA: Newbury House.

BIRDSONG, D. 1992, Ultimate attainment in second language acquisition. *Language* 68, 706–55.

BLEY-VROMAN, R. 1990, The logical problem of foreign language learning. *Linguistic Analysis* 20, 3–49.

BROWN, R. and HANLON, C. 1970, Derivational complexity and order of acquisition in child speech. In J. HAYES (ed.) *Cognition and the Development of Language* (pp. 11–53). New York: Wiley.

CHOMSKY, N. 1981, *Lectures on Government and Binding*. Dordrecht: Foris.

CLAHSEN, H. 1990, The comparative study of first and second language development. *Studies in Second Language Acquisition* 12, 135–54.

CLARK, E. 1987, The principle of contrast: A constraint on language acquisition. In B. MACWHINNEY (ed.) *Mechanisms of Language Acquisition* (pp. 1–34). Hillsdale, NJ: Lawrence Erlbaum.

COPPIETERS, R. 1987, Competence differences between native and fluent non-native speakers. *Language* 63, 544–73.

DAY, E. and SHAPSON, S. 1991, Integrating formal and functional approaches to language teaching in French immersion: An experimental approach. *Language Learning* 41, 25–58.

DEMETRAS, M., POST, K. and SNOW, C. 1986, Feedback to first language learners: The role of repetitions and clarification questions. *Journal of Child Language* 13, 275–92.

DOUGHTY, C. 1991, Second language instruction does make a difference: Evidence from an empirical study of second language relativization. *Studies in Second Language Acquisition* 13, 431–69.

ECKMAN, F., BELL, L. and NELSON, D. 1988, On the generalization of relative clause instruction in the acquisition of English as a second language. *Applied Linguistics* 9, 1–20.

FARGHALY, A. 1982, Subject pronoun deletion rule in Egyptian Arabic. In S. GAMAL and R. BOWERS (eds) *Discourse Analysis: Theory and Application: Proceedings of the Second National Symposium on Linguistics and English Training* (pp. 60–69). Cairo: Center for Developing English Language Teaching, Ain Shams University.

FELIX, S. 1985, More evidence on competing cognitive systems. *Second Language Research* 1, 47–72.

FLYNN, S. 1989, The role of the head-initial/head-final parameter in the acquisition of English relative clauses by adult Spanish and Japanese speakers. In S. GASS and J. SCHACHTER (eds) *Linguistic Perspectives on Second Language Acquisition* (pp. 306–326). Cambridge: Cambridge University Press.

GASS, S. 1982, From theory to practice. In M. HINES and W. RUTHERFORD (eds) *On TESOL '81* (pp. 129–139). Washington, DC: TESOL.

HARLEY, B. 1989, Functional grammar in French immersion: A classroom experiment. *Applied Linguistics* 10, 331–59.

HIGGS, T. and CLIFFORD, R. 1982, The push toward communication. In T. HIGGS (ed.) *Curriculum, Competence, and the Foreign Language Teacher* (pp. 57–79). Skokie, IL: National Textbook Co.

HIRSH-PASEK, K., TREIMAN, R. and SCHNEIDERMAN, M. 1984, Brown and Hanlon revisited: Mothers' sensitivity to ungrammatical forms. *Journal of Child Language* 11, 81–8.

IOUP, G., BOUSTAGUI, E., EL TIGI, M. and MOSELLE, M. 1994, Reexamining the critical period hypothesis: A case study of successful SLA in a naturalistic environment. *Studies in Second Language Acquisition* 16, 73–98.

JOHNSON, J. and NEWPORT, E. 1989, Critical period effects in second language learning: The influence of maturational state on the acquisition of ESL. *Cognitive Psychology* 21, 60–99.

KRASHEN, S, 1980, The theoretical and practical relevance of simple codes in second language acquisition. In R. SCARCELLA and S. KRASHEN (eds) *Research in Second Language Acquisition* (pp. 7–18). Rowley, MA: Newbury House.

KRASHEN, S. 1981, *Second Language Acquisition and Second Language Learning*. Oxford: Pergamon Press.

LENNEBERG, E. 1967, *Biological Foundations of Language*. New York: John Wiley.

LONG, M. 1990, Maturational constraints on language development. *Studies in Second Language Acquisition* 12, 251–85.

MACWHINNEY, B. 1987, The competition model. In B. MACWHINNEY (ed.) *Mechanisms of Language Acquisition* (pp. 249–308). Hillsdale, NJ: Lawrence Erlbaum.

McLAUGHLIN, B. 1978, The Monitor Model, some methodological considerations. *Language Learning* 28, 309–22.

NOVOA, L., FEIN, D. and OBLER, L. 1989, Talent in foreign languages: A case study. In L. OBLER and D. FEIN (eds) *The Exceptional Brain: The Neuropsychology of Talent and Special Abilities* (pp. 294–302). New York: Guilford Press.

OBLER, L. 1989, Exceptional second language learners. In S. GASS, C. MADDEN, D. PRESTON and L. SELINKER (eds) *Variation in Second Language Acquisition: Psycholinguistic Issues* (pp. 141–59). Clevedon: Multilingual Matters.

OSMAN, M. 1990, The syntax and logical form of *wh*-interrogatives in Cairene Egyptian Arabic. Unpublished doctoral dissertation, University of Washington.

OYAMA, S. 1976, A sensitive period in the acquisition of a non-native phonological system. *Journal of Psycholinguistic Research* 5, 261–85.

PATKOWSKI, M. 1980, The sensitive period for acquisition of syntax in a second language. *Language Learning* 30, 449–72.

PAVESI, M. 1986, Markedness, discourse modes, and relative clause formation in a formal and informal context. *Studies in Second Language Acquisition* 8, 138–55.

PENFIELD, W. and ROBERTS, L. 1959, *Speech and Brain Mechanisms*. New York: Atheneum Press.

PIENEMANN, M. 1984, Psychological constraints on the teachability of languages. *Studies in Second Language Acquisition* 6, 186–214.

PINKER, S. 1984, *Language Learnability and Language Development*. Cambridge, MA: Harvard University Press.

— 1987, The bootstrapping problem in language acquisition. In B. MACWHINNEY (ed.) *Mechanisms of Language Acquisition*. Hillsdale, NJ: Lawrence Erlbaum.

RUTHERFORD, W. 1988, Aspects of pedagogical grammar. In W. RUTHERFORD and M. SHARWOOD SMITH (eds) *Grammar and Second Language Teaching* (pp. 171–85). New York: Newbury House.

SCARCELLA, R. 1983, Discourse accent in second language performance. In S. GASS and L. SELINKER (eds) *Language Transfer and Language Learning* (pp. 306–26). Rowley, MA: Newbury House.

SCHACHTER, J. 1986, Three approaches to the study of input. *Language Learning* 36, 211–25.

— 1989, Testing a proposed universal. In S. GASS and J. SCHACHTER (eds) *Linguistic Perspectives on Second Language Acquisition* (pp. 73–88). Cambridge: Cambridge University Press.

SCHMIDT, R. 1983, Interaction, acculturation, and the acquisition of communicative competence: A case study of an adult. In N. WOLFSON and E. JUDD (eds) *Sociolinguistics and Language Acquisition* (pp. 137–74). Rowley, MA: Newbury House.

SCHMIDT, R. and FROTA, S. 1986, Developing basic conversational ability in a second language: A case study of an adult learner of Portuguese. In R. DAY (ed.) *'Talking to Learn': Conversation in Second Language Acquisition* (pp. 237–326). Rowley, MA: Newbury House.

SCHWARTZ, B. 1986, The epistemological status of second language acquisition. *Second Language Research* 2, 120–59.
— 1993, On explicit and negative data effecting and affecting competence and linguistic behavior. *Studies in Second Language Acquisition* 15, 147–63.
SCHNEIDERMAN, E. and DESMARAIS, C. 1988a, A neuropsychological substrate for talent in second language acquisition. In L. OBLER and D. FEIN (eds) *The Exceptional Brain: Neuropsychology of Talent and Special Abilities*. New York: Guilford Press.
— 1988b, The talented language learner: Some preliminary findings. *Second Language Research* 4, 91–109.
SCOVEL, T 1981, The recognition of foreign accents in English and its implications for psycholinguistic theories of language acquisition. In J. SCAVARD and L. LAFORGE (eds) *Proceedings of the Fifth Congress of AILA* (pp. 389–401). Laval, Canada: University of Laval Press.
SELINKER, L. 1972, Interlanguage. *International Review of Applied Linguistics* 10, 209–31.
SHARWOOD SMITH, M. 1981, Consciousness-raising and second language learning. *Applied Linguistics* 2, 159–68.
— 1991, Speaking to many minds: On the relevance of different types of language information for the L2 learner. *Second Language Research* 7, 118–33.
SMITH, N. and TSIMPLE, I 1991, Linguistic modularity? A case study of a 'savant' linguist. *Lingua* 84, 315–51.
SORACE, A. 1993, Incomplete vs. divergent representations of unaccusativity in non-native grammars of Italian. *Second Language Research* 9, 22–48.
TRAHEY, M. and WHITE, L. 1993, Positive evidence and preemption in the second language classroom. *Studies in Second Language Acquisition* 15, 181–204.
VAN PATTEN, B. 1988, How juries get hung: Problems with the evidence for a focus on form in teaching. *Language Learning* 38, 243–60.
WHITE, L. 1981, The responsibility of grammatical theory to acquisitional data. In N. HORNSTEIN and D. LIGHTFOOT (eds) *Explanation in Linguistics* (pp. 241–71). London: Longman.
— 1989, The principle of adjacency in second language acquisition: Do L2 learners observe the subset principle? In S. GASS. and J. SCHACHTER (eds) *Linguistic Perspectives on Second Language Acquisition* (pp. 134–58). Cambridge: Cambridge University Press.
— (1991), Adverb placement in second language acquisition: Some effects of positive and negative evidence in the classroom. *Second Language Research* 7, 133–61.
— (1992), On triggering data in L2 acquisition: A reply to Schwartz and Gibala-Ryzak. *Second Language Research* 8, 120–37.
WHITE, L. and GENESEE, F. 1993, How native is near-native? The issue of age and ultimate attainment in the acquisition of a second language. Unpublished manuscript, McGill University.
WHITE, L., SPADA, N., LIGHTBOWN, P. and RANTA, L. 1991, Input enhancement and L2 question formation. *Applied Linguistics* 12, 416–32.
WONG-FILLMORE, L. 1979, Individual differences in second language acquisition. In E. FILLMORE, D. KEMPLER and W. WANG (eds) *Individual Differences in Language Ability and Language Behavior* (pp. 203–28). New York: Academic Press.

5 Some Critical Remarks on the Phonological Component

ZSOLT LENGYEL

Introduction

The Critical Period Hypothesis (CPH) relates to both the first (mother tongue) and the second (or foreign) language acquisitional processes. While some researchers in the areas of the linguistic sciences and speech behaviour fully accept the CPH, others deny its correctness or existence. Regardless of whether they accept it or not, they all tend to appeal to biological, neurological and sociopsychological arguments either for or against the CPH. A detailed discussion of these various factors is provided by Larsen-Freeman & Long (1991).

To those who accept it, the CPH entails certain constraints. In the case of first language acquisition, it implies that if first language learning begins beyond the end of the critical period, the result will be a highly impoverished overall language competence. The CPH does not necessarily apply to second (or foreign) language acquisition in such a global fashion. Thus, it has been suggested by some that the critical period affects only certain aspects of second (or foreign) language acquisition, notably phonology. To be more precise, it has been claimed that phonological proficiency (pronunciation) can attain a native-like quality only if the second (or foreign) language learning begins before the end of the critical period — i.e. not later than 6 or 12 years of age depending on the specific terms of any given formulation of the CPH (for more details see Scovel, 1988: 164–86).

Several counter-arguments have been developed against the CPH (see, e.g. Van Els *et al.*, 1984; Ellis, 1985; McLaughlin, 1987). The present study wishes to raise some doubts regarding its phonological claims level in relation to the process of second (or foreign) language acquisition.

Proponents of the CPH are inclined to think that children before puberty are 'good phoneticians', whereas adolescents and adults are often deemed 'good grammarians and semanticists'. Such general statements suffer from several shortcomings. I will mention just two such.

First, we must draw attention to language typology. It is only common sense to suggest that a given language function can be expressed in one language at the phonological level, and in another language at a different linguistic level. It is also known that the same phonological event can expound several language functions depending on the language concerned.

The nasalisation of vowels in the French language is seen as a commonplace; it has a 'normal' functional profile within French phonology — having a general role in lexical differentiation. This, no doubt, explains why it is acquired by French children in early childhood. In the Hungarian language nasalisation is also used but as one of the tools for the production of 'aristocratic speech'. That is, this phenomenon has an essentially sociolinguistic value, which is undoubtedly why it can be handled by Hungarian children only after their early teens. Thus, the same phonological phenomenon serves in one case as a 'normal language tool' and is acquired very early, whereas in another case it functions as a sociolinguistic tool and is acquired (learned) only later, during adolescence.

The claim that children younger than 12 or 6 years of age are 'good phoneticians' does not seem to be supported in this form either by the practice or the theory of second (or foreign) language acquisition. Objections to this claim include the following:

(1) Foreign language teachers' experience could be brought up here as a practical objection. According to this experience children are very different in terms of successful acquisition of phonological skills in second (or foreign) language courses.
(2) A more theory-based counter-argument stems from the notion of individual learning strategies. It would be strange to deny the existence of several kinds of language learning strategies governing the acquisitional and learning processes at the phonological level as well. Since strategies exist, they imply individual differences. These differences can or, rather, must influence the quality of knowledge, the rate of the acquisition and other factors in the language learning process.
(3) Proponents of the CPH have alleged that the capacity to recognise foreign accents recognition is not developed before the ages of 10 to 12 (see Scovel, 1988: 109–11). Neither the experience of early bilingualism nor the practice of early second language teaching seem to lend support

to this statement. Bearing in mind the more-or-less accepted assumption regarding the asymmetry between production and reception (that is, the assumption that receptive skills usually precede productive skills in both L1 and L2), it does not seem very plausible to consider these particular receptive skills (the recognition of foreign accents) as skills that are more likely to be developed during or after puberty.

In what follows I shall present some results of two foreign language learning experiments carried out among Hungarian children. The first is related to receptive skills; that is, to the recognition of foreign accent. The second sets out to study phonological productive skills, also within the framework of the learning processes of a foreign language.

Perception of a Foreign Accent

The experiment

The experiment involved 10 test-words as follows:

(1) Hungarian words (H): *mama* ('mummy'), *papa* ('daddy');
(2) Russian words (R): *mama* ('mummy'), *papa* ('daddy'), *peresol* ('crossed');
(3) possible H: *bivu, peresol;*
(4) impossible H: *sklat;*
(5) possible R: *bivu, sklat.*

In a sense we can say that five HWs and five RWs were present in the test respectively. All the words were recorded by female native speakers.

The participants (aged 6–8 years) had the task of detecting which words were uttered by a Hungarian and which ones by a Russian speaker. The arrangement of words was as follows:

(1) *mama* (R)
(2) *peresol* (H)
(3) *mama* (H)
(4) *peresol* (R)
(5) *papa* (R)
(6) *sklat* (H)
(7) *papa* (H)
(8) *sklat* (R)
(9) *bivu* (R)
(10) *bivu* (H)

Such an arrangement of words would diminish the role of chance. Exposure by pairs (*papa* (R) – *papa* (H), *mama* (H) – *mama* (R) etc.) might easily have resulted in a level of correct response rate of 50% without this result having any particular significance.

Some phonetic characteristics of test-words

(1) Differences at feature level between vowels: *mama, papa* (H) – *mama, papa* (R). In the Hungarian language [a] is a labial; in Russian it is an illabial sound.
(2) Differences at feature level between consonants: *peresol* (H) – *peresol* (R). The Russian sound [ʃ] is an alveolo-palatal fricative; the Hungarian [ʃ] is an post-alveolar one.
(3 Segment-level difference: *bivu* (R) – *bivu* (H). The Hungarian [i] is a palatal; the Russian [i] is a velar sound.
(4) Suprasegmental-level difference: *sklat* (H) – *sklat* (R). Hungarian phonotactic rules, unlike Russian phonotactic rules, prohibit consonant-clusters word-initially.

The stimulus word-forms have phonetic differences in addition to those already mentioned. For instance, the Russian [p] and [r] are palatalised sounds. But these and other differences do not play such an important role as those detailed above.

The experiment tries to shed light on three interrelated questions:

(1) the phonetic characteristics and degrees of foreign accent recognition;
(2) how this recognition is affected by biological age;
(3) how this recognition is affected by the time-span of second language learning.

In the experiment two factors ('biological age' and 'number of years of second language learning') cannot be separated. Table 5.1 summarises this situation. According to the traditional interpretation of the CPH, two kinds of results could be expected:

(1) On the one hand, if 10–12 years of age is accepted as the upper limit of the critical period, then the correctness of recognition side should gradually improve, as all the age-groups are within the critical period. On the other hand, phonetic perception skills are obviously improved by learning experiences. Taking into account these facts, an improvement can be predicted in the results.
(2) If 6 years of age is considered to be the final point of the critical period, then we should expect either stagnation or just a very moderate improvement in results.

Table 5.1

Biological age	*Years of study*
6 years	0.5
7 years	1.5
8 years	2.5

Another important point of interest in the results is the extent to which there are differences in phonetic perception caused by featural, segmental or suprasegmental factors respectively.

The results of the experiment

Table 5.2 shows the results from the point of view of the incorrect solutions (in order of stimulus presentation). Group 1 has been learning a foreign language for half a year, Group 2 for one and a half years, Group 3 for two and a half years.

Allowing for a 5% margin of error, the stimulus words can be divided into two groups:

(1) Children recognise correctly the stimuli: *papa* (H), *papa* (R), *mama* (H), *mama* (R), *sklat* (R), *bivu* (R), *peresol* (R). (There is only one exception: in Group 3, where the recognition error rate for Russian mama is 11.80%.)
(2) Stimuli *peresol* (H), *bivu* (H) and *sklat* (H) are recognised with a varying error rate.

Table 5.2 Percentages of incorrect solutions

	Group 1	*Group 2*	*Group 3*
1. *mama* (R)	3.14	1.82	11.80
2. *peresol* (H)	23.36	28.55	19.23
3. *mama* (H)	3.36	1.42	3.31
4. *peresol* (R)	4.72	2.78	6.97
5. *papa* (R)	2.08	4.28	6.90
6. *sklat* (H)	26.23	31.99	29.73
7. *papa* (H)	6.61	2.13	0.76
8. *sklat* (R)	3.08	5.42	4.94
9. *bivu* (R)	2.20	1.65	0.81
10. *bivu* (H)	24.72	19.92	15.13

The results can be examined in the perspective of stimuli pairs. Some clarificatory remarks on this form of presentation are in order here.

(1) Each member of a given pair of stimuli elicits a different level of accurate recognition. The member which elicits more accurate recognition is underlined and printed in bold (e.g. the recognition of **papa** (R) in Group 1 is better than that of *papa* (H)).

(2) The difference between the recognition rate of the members of one and the same stimulus pair is very important. If this rate is low (i.e. not more than 5%), then one can assume that it is due to correct phonetic analysis carried out by the children. If this rate is high, then one can infer some problems with the phonetic perception of the less frequently recognised member of the stimulus pair.

The results of the three groups are similar regarding the percentage of correct recognition. The stimuli correctly recognised within the 5–6% error limit are common across all groups (see Table 5.2).

Some further points worthy of note include the following:

(1) Some of the correctly recognised stimuli constitute homonymic pairs: *papa* (H) – *papa* (R), *mama* (H) – *mama* (R). We have a strong suspicion that the phonetic recognition in these cases is supported by the semantic level also.

(2) Children recognise correctly the stimuli *peresol* (R), *bivu* (R) and *sklat* (R), if these stimuli have the Russian phonetic characteristics. The Hungarian phonetic shape of these stimuli is not supported at all by the semantic level. This leads us to think that children tend to qualify a given acoustic stimulus not supported by the semantic level as a phonetic event of a foreign language, even if this acoustic stimulus is formed by the phonological rules of their mother tongue.

We are inclined by the foregoing to believe that children activate all the available linguistic levels to gain their goal during problem-solving tasks. There is no reason to assume that children (like linguists) try to separate linguistic levels in the foreign language learning process. On the contrary, just the opposite is the case. (The separation mentioned above is rare; compare the role of pragmatics in the learning of animal names by children in a foreign language.) In this respect the separation of different linguistic levels is a bit artificial, or at least it is questionable whether it reflects the real situation or process.

Table 5.3 shows the level of correct recognition of the various stimulus pairs. The following points are worth commenting on in this connection.

Table 5.3 Percentage differences of correct recognition of stimulus pairs

Group	*H*	*R*	*Percentage difference*
1.	*papa*	*papa*	1.99
	mama	*mama*	4.42
	peresol	*peresol*	14.93
	bivu	*bivu*	22.56
	sklat	*sklat*	23.15
2.	*mama*	*mama*	0.4
	papa	*papa*	2.15
	bivu	*bivu*	18.26
	peresol	*peresol*	25.78
	sklat	*sklat*	26.57
3.	*papa*	*papa*	6.14
	mama	*mama*	8.46
	bivu	*bivu*	14.20
	peresol	*peresol*	15.59
	sklat	*sklat*	24.82

(1) It is easy to recognise either the Hungarian or the Russian form of *mama* and *papa*. The percentage of their correct recognition is very close, it is not more than 5%. Whether the Russian or the Hungarian member is more frequently recognised in these circumstances is of no significance.Recognition in these cases is supported both at the phonetic level and at the semantic level. This 'double' help is equally well used by all age-groups.

(2) It is a commonly noted fact that children tend to regard a speech event as a foreign language one, if this event is not supported by the semantics of the mother tongue. This no doubt accounts for the difficulty experienced by the subjects in recognising possible and impossible Hungarian words.

(3) It is also commonly accepted that suprasegmental (phonotactic) rules seem to have a very important role in phonetic perception. One notes in this connection that each group has the biggest problem with the recognition of the stimulus *sklat* uttered in accordance with the rules of Hungarian segmental phonetics. This may be caused by the fact that the acoustic stimulus, since it does not conform to the phonotactic rules

of the mother tongue, does not even get to the short-term memory which is responsible for segmentation. (Of course one needs to ask whether this is general fact or a problem appearing just in this experiment. In this experiment stimuli breaking the phonotactic rules of mother tongue could be recognised as a foreign language event.)

(4) It is interesting to follow the fate of the stimuli *bivu* and *peresol*: *bivu* contains a velar [i], *peresol* a velar [ʃ]. Both sounds are very typical Russian ones and at the same time very unusual for the Hungarian ear.
    (i) The two elder groups can apparently better use the information provided by the vowel in question, whereas for younger ones the consonant seems to make the solution easier.
    (ii) For the eldest group the segmental and suprasegmental difficulties are relatively well separated (compare the differences in percentage: 6.14, 8.46, 14.20, 15.59, 24.82). For younger children both the most difficult segmental and the suprasegmental problems are equal (compare the result of *bivu* 22.56 and *sklat* 23.15 in Group 1, and that of *peresol* 25.78 and *sklat* 26.57 in Group 2).

(5) In connection with the stimuli papa and mama it is worth noting that during the recognition process the elder age group seemed to apply the strategy 'this is Hungarian, so the other one is not'. This is less characteristic of the younger groups. The question arises whether this is a consequence of the language teaching method (i.e. does the method make children view the foreign language through their mother tongue?). It may, on the other hand, be a spontaneous process whereby learners approach the foreign language through the intermediary of their mother tongue whatever the teaching method used.

Summarising this experiment it is worth calling attention to two things:

(1) The phonological level is not a monolithic component for children. It has different peculiarities depending on whether recognition is directed to a featural, a segmental or a suprasegmental element.

(2) Age-related differences emerged but they were not so significant that they should be attributed to the facts mentioned above.

Production Experiment

This experiment was carried out among 9-year-old Hungarian children without any foreign language experience. The experiment had several goals but I shall deal here with just one of them.

The experiment

The children involved in the experiment were given the task of repeating recorded Russian words as accurately as they could. Thus, in fact, the experimental task required some elements of perceptive and reproductive skills as well as productive skills *stricto sensu*. However, the focus in what follows will be on the productive dimension.

There were 550 stimulus words, which were divided into 55 series, each of which contained ten words. Each series was attempted by ten children. Accordingly, the resultant data-set comprised 5500 items, and these constitute the basis of our corpus. Three native speakers were asked to judge the correctness of pronunciation of the items in question. The native speakers had only one option: either to accept or to reject a given pronunciation. In each case the decision of the majority of the judges was accepted, whether it was unanimous or not.

The phonetic characteristics of the test words

The test-words reflected two peculiarities of Russian phonetics which are totally absent in the Hungarian language:

(1) the word-initial consonant cluster (a phonotactic difference between the two languages in question);

(2) the palatalisation of consonants.

The test-words began with the consonant clusters [bd], [bl], [br]. As has already been made clear, the consonant cluster is impossible word-initially in the Hungarian language (with the exception of some loanwords). In the present discussion I shall briefly analyse what emerged in respect of just one of the stimulus words in question: *bdet*.

The result of the experiment

Based on the judgment of the native speakers, the subjects' attempts to pronounce *bdet* can be divided into two subgroups:

(1) 25% of the pronunciation attempts were correct.

(2) 75% were incorrect.

There were three types of error:

(i) *pdet* instead of *bdet* (i.e. replacing the sound [b] with [p];

(ii) *bridet* or *blidet* instead of *bdet* (i.e. adding in a [ri] or [li] syllable to the initial segment of the stimulus);

(iii) a highly heterogeneous range of other miscellaneous mistakes.

There was a more or less proportional distribution of items among the three subtypes mentioned above.

Here I shall deal with just two subtypes. It is important to emphasise that errors along the same lines occur with regard to other stimuli too. Therefore the analysis and the consequences below have a value which extends well beyond the single case of *bdet*.

The pronunciation of the stimulus *bdet* in the form of either *bridet* or *blidet* reveals that the subjects concerned perceive the two phonetic peculiarities of the Russian language in question, namely the phonotactic rule (consonant-cluster in word-initial position) and the palatalisation of the sound [d]. Not only can they perceive the phonotactic rule, but they can also produce it. On the other hand, whereas they can perceive the palatalisation of the sound [d], they cannot produce it. More precisely, under the effect of the acoustic stimulus the children appear to search for a solution among the 'most palatalised' sounds of the mother tongue, i.e. of the Hungarian language, and without a doubt the 'most appropriate sounds' from this point of view are [r] and [l]. The strategy applied by these children to solve this problem seems to be as follows: 'this is something totally new; try to reflect it in an exaggerated way'. As they have no foreign language experience, they choose as a means of reflection the phonetic elements of their mother tongue which are closest to the phonetic event of the foreign language.

These children — owing either to their weak perceptive or to their weak productive skills — are unable to produce accurately the phonetic peculiarities in question, but they 'feel' something. To express this subtle feeling they turn to the most general (therefore a very neutral) phonetic feature of their mother tongue (i.e. of the Hungarian language). Hungarian consonants can be either voiced or voiceless; this being their most essential characteristic feature. The strategy standing behind this solution can be formulated as follows: 'it is a strange phonetic event but one can solve it within the frames of one's mother tongue'. (Later these children may become very sceptical language learners. They may question the correctness of a given foreign language structure or form all the time, if the latter are very different from their mother tongue's structures.) Handling the peculiarities of the foreign language structures with the help of the mother tongue can of course appear, in addition to the phonetic level, at the morphological, syntactic, etc. levels.

Conclusion

Both the theoretical arguments rehearsed above and the reported experimental results run counter to the notion that the phonological component of the CPH can be treated as a monolith. Accordingly, the view that children younger than 6 or 12 are in some global sense 'good phoneticians' must be rejected as at the very least over-simplistic. The following gaps in our state of knowledge in this context would benefit from further consideration and further research.

(1) We do not have sufficient knowledge about how the acquisitional process proceeds at the phonological level. We need more information about which elements (features, segments, suprasegmental features) are acquired easily and which create difficulties, and to what extent these difficulties are influenced by the native language of the foreign language learner.

(2) We do not have sufficient knowledge about the strategies applied by children during the acquisition of foreign language phonology either. The deployment of different learning strategies by different learners would appear to have at least two consequences:
   (i) Different strategies will imply different individual language competence outcomes.
   (ii) It is reasonable to suppose that there are some connections between strategies used by one and the same language learner at several language levels.

References

ELLIS, R. 1985, *Understanding Second Language Acquisition*. Oxford: Oxford University Press.

LARSEN-FREEMAN, D. and LONG, M.H. 1991, *An Introduction to Second Language Acquisition Research*. London and New York: Longman

McLAUGHLIN, B. 1987, *Theories of Second-Language Learning*. London: Edward Arnold.

SCOVEL, T. 1988, *A Time to Speak. A Psycholinguistic Inquiry into the Critical Period for Human Speech*. Rowley, MA: Newbury House.

VAN ELS, T., BONGAERTS, T., EXTRA, G., VAN OS, C. and JANSSEN-DIETEN, A. 1984, *Applied Linguistics and the Learning and Teaching of Foreign Languages*. London: Edward Arnold.

6 Is There an Age-Factor for Universal Grammar?

GITA MARTOHARDJONO and SUZANNE FLYNN

Introduction

In the past decade, many arguments have been made for a critical period or perhaps multiple critical periods for all aspects of the language acquisition process. In this chapter, we discuss some research findings which strongly suggest that there are at least two areas of language which are not affected by a critical period. Both derive from the biologically endowed faculty for language and are: (i) the innate principles and parameters of Universal Grammar (UG) governing the acquisition of syntax; and (ii) the biologically determined sensory abilities for the development of sound systems.

To assume this position is not to deny the fact that there may be certain differences between adults and children in language learning; however, we argue that these differences do not of themselves reflect the role of the biologically endowed faculty for language which we believe should be of central focus to inquiry into language acquisition in general and into critical periods in particular. We begin in the first section with a brief outline of the role UG principles and parameters play in the acquisition of syntax. We then discuss evidence from certain areas in the acquisition of syntax which do not show critical period effects. In the second section we consider aspects of the acquisition of sound systems — in particular, the substrate for speech cognition — and we present evidence indicating that basic competence in this area remains accessible to the adult learner as well.

The Language Faculty in the Domain of Syntax

In order to make our claims clear, we first have to consider two issues. One has to do with what we assume to be involved in language acquisition in general; the other with what we mean by a biologically endowed faculty for language.

Clearly, the acquisition of language is not a unidimensional process but a complex system determined by the interaction of several different processes that occur simultaneously. Consider, for example, what the children have to do in order to learn only one aspect of language, namely the lexicon: not only must they learn the pairing of sound and meaning particular to their language, they must also deduce the categorial information for each lexical item, i.e. whether it is a noun, a verb etc. In addition they must learn the grammatical information pertinent to each lexical item, i.e. its subcategorisation features. For example, children learning English must learn that certain verbs, like *enjoy*, take a gerund; that others, like *want*, take the infinitive; and that still others, like *prefer*, can take both the infinitive and the gerund. Clearly this is a complex process, and presumably the children acquire this type of information by paying attention to their linguistic environment. Thus, certain aspects of language are learnable because they can be induced from positive evidence. In addition, however, the child also comes to know aspects of grammar which are 'unlearned', in the sense that they cannot be derived given the nature of the evidence available to the child. These, we argue, include syntactic principles and parameters provided by the biologically endowed faculty for language, or UG.

Let us very briefly consider some of the arguments leading to the innate UG hypothesis, as first formulated in Chomsky (1968). It is well known that a child attains the complex system of language despite a deficiency of language data on at least four levels[1].

Firstly, the speech that the child hears does not uniformly consist of complete grammatical sentences, but of utterances replete with pauses, false starts and slips of the tongue. Secondly, the language that the child hears is finite; yet the child comes to be capable of both producing *and* understanding utterances that go far beyond those that were ever heard in childhood. Thirdly, people attain knowledge of the structure of their language for which no evidence is available in the data they are exposed to as children. For example, children are not systematically informed that certain utterances are ungrammatical or that some are paraphrases of other utterances, or that other utterances are ambiguous. And finally, the exposure to the language is not uniform for all children; yet children worldwide acquire their first languages with amazing regularity in spite of the differences in background and intelligence. All of this is attained in a fairly remarkably short period of time, without much effort or conscious thought, and with only a narrow range of the logically possible errors that could be committed. Such facts demand an explanation. In fact, one is logically led to positing a biological domain-specific organ that can account for these and many other facts about language acquisition. This domain specific-language faculty makes language acquisition possible by reducing the learner's hypothesis space regarding what makes a possible human language.

As an example of the type of knowledge made available by UG, consider the sentence in (1):

(1) He makes John's lunch.

It is clear to any native speaker of English that in this sentence *He* and *John* cannot be coreferential. Logically, there is no reason why this should be so. Two observations have been made about this fact: one is that all children learning English as their L1 come to know it without explicit instruction; the other is that this restriction on coreference holds true in all languages. It is to account for the knowledge of facts like these that the language faculty, and in particular UG, is argued to be innate. UG is composed of principles that universally characterise all languages, like the one disallowing coreference in (1) and known in UG Theory as Principle B of the Binding Theory.

Some UG principles have slightly different instantiations across languages. For example, all languages have a principal branching direction; they can vary to the left, as for Japanese, or to the right, as for English. Such differences are accounted for in terms of parameters. In this particular example, for the same principle, namely Branching Direction, Japanese is parameterised as left-branching, and English as right-branching. In order for this system to work, children must be exposed to a particular linguistic environment to determine whether their language is left-branching or right-branching. Some of the evidence we present later in this chapter pertains to this particular parameter.

So far, then, we have mentioned at least three aspects of the language acquisition process which presumably occur simultaneously. These are schematised in Figure 6.1. To construct a particular grammar, for example, that of English, a child must have access to the language faculty with its principles and parameters, a lexicon, and language-specific rules. Important to note in this regard is that to acquire language, two types of data-driven 'learning' are involved. One has to do with the setting of parameters, which necessitates exposure to the relevant data for a particular language in order to determine the parametric values. Technically, this involves *deductive* learning which derives from the language

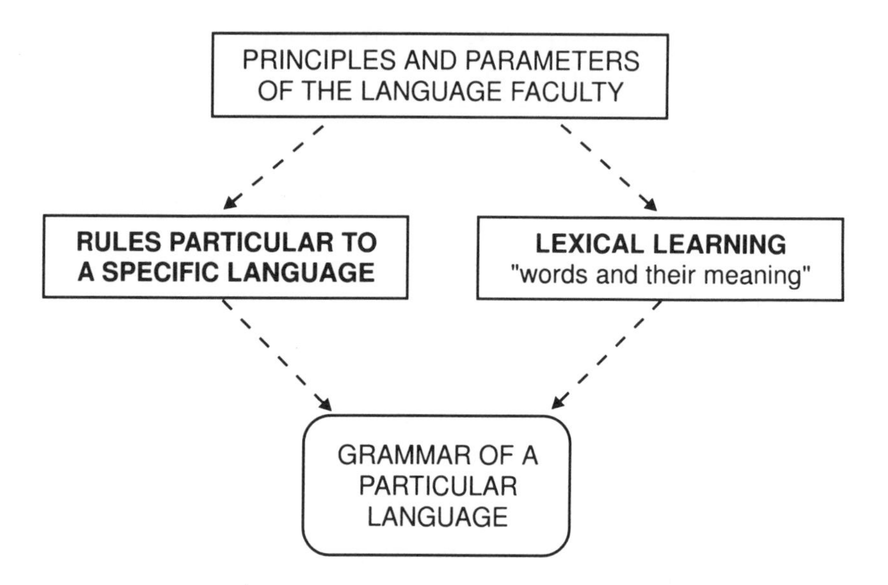

Figure 6.1 Process of language-particular grammar construction

faculty. Another type of learning — e.g. of the lexicon and idiosyncratic rules — may in addition involve an *inductive* procedure, and may therefore be dependent on cognitive faculties rather than the language faculty. What we hope to show in this section is that, while the question of a critical period for the inductive processes of language acquisition remains open, there seems to be no such period for the deductive processes, particularly in the area of syntax.

Evidence from L2 acquisition

The most direct way to test the existence of a critical period for UG principles and parameters is to test whether they are still accessible in adulthood, and more specifically, whether adult second language learners have knowledge of UG principles in the L2. Importantly, we want to test principles which are instantiated differently in the first and second languages respectively. As we have seen, one such situation arises with parameterisation, that is, if the L1 and L2 choose different values for the same parameter. Another situation is that of principles which are triggered only under certain circumstances, which hold for the L2 but not L1 (see Martohardjono & Gair, 1993). This arises in the case of Chinese and Indonesian adults learning English as a second language. Specifically, the structure under consideration is question-formation. As shown in (2) below, languages differ in the ways they form questions.

(2) Two types of question-formation

English:	Chinese:
Whom Do You Like?	*Ni Xihuan Shei?*
	you like who

In English, the question word appears at the beginning of the sentence, a result ascribed in UG theory to 'syntantic *wh*-movement'. Many other languages, like Chinese and Japanese, lack this type of movement, and in such languages the question word appears '*in situ*' as seen in the Chinese example in (2). An examination of languages with syntactic movement has yielded the observation that this type of movement is subject to a universal principle which restricts the domain out of which a wh-word may be moved. This is illustrated in Figure 6.2.

A. THE GIRL WHO HAD A STOMACH ACHE ATE A COOKIE

B. WHAT DID THE GIRL [WHO HAD A STOMACH ACHE] EAT ___?

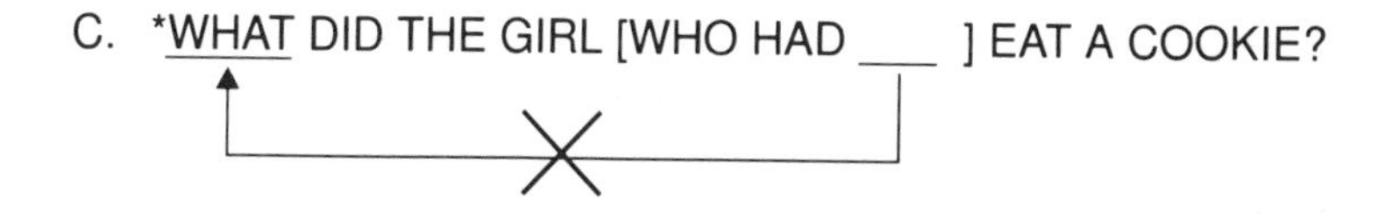

Figure 6.2 Restrictions on syntactic movement

Consider first sentence A, which contains two noun phrases. Logically it should be possible to question either of these nouns and for *in situ* languages this is in fact the case. However, as one sees in sentences B and C, there is a marked difference in acceptability between the two questions when movement is involved. Questioning the word *cookie* results in an acceptable sentence. In contrast, questioning the expression *stomach ache*, as in C, results in an unacceptable sentence. This effect has been ascribed to a principle called Subjacency (Chomsky, 1973) which, together with some other principles, forms the more general principle of Constraints on Syntactic Movement. Notice that sentences B and C are structurally similar in that they are permutations of the same sentence A. Both have the form of a question containing a relative clause. The critical difference between B and C is that in B, the acceptable sentence, the questioned word originates in the main clause, while in C, the unacceptable one, the questioned word originates in the relative clause. It is of course highly unlikely that language learners, whether they be children or adults, are ever explicitly instructed about facts such as these. Yet any native speaker of English can detect this difference and tell you that B is fine, while C is not.

Importantly, in languages without syntactic movement, the equivalent of sentence C is grammatical. This is because Subjacency is only triggered when syntactic movement occurs, and since these languages do not have this type of movement in questions (recall that the question words remain *in situ*), Subjacency does not apply. The interesting question that arises, then, is the following: How do adult learners who are native speakers of a language without syntactic *wh*-movement treat sentences like C when learning English? More concretely, do native speakers of Chinese, for example, know that questioning a noun inside a relative clause is ungrammatical in English even though it is allowed in Chinese? Recall that knowledge of this constraint is provided by UG. A Critical Period Hypothesis for UG principles would therefore predict that native speakers of *in situ* languages learning English beyond a certain age (presumably after puberty) will not recognise the ungrammaticality of sentences like C in English. This is precisely what Martohardjono (1993) set out to investigate. In what follows we will review the relevant part of the results obtained in that study.

Martohardjono (1993) presented a variety of ungrammatical sentences in English, such as C in Figure 6.2, to two groups of adult learners of English who were native speakers of Chinese and Indonesian, two languages which do not have syntactic movement in question-formation, and hence two languages where movement constraints are not instantiated. Only subjects who had started learning English after the age of 15 were included. In addition to the extractions out of relative clauses illustrated in Figure 6.2, two other types of structures were included, for which movement constraints also hold: extractions out of Sentential Subjects and extractions out of Adjunct Clauses. Examples are given in Figure 6.3.

Table 6.1 shows mean percentages of unacceptable sentences which were *correctly* rejected as 'ungrammatical' by the Indonesian and the Chinese groups. It is clear from these figures that both groups showed solid knowledge of the movement constraints for all the structures tested. Martohardjono concluded from this that UG principles which are not

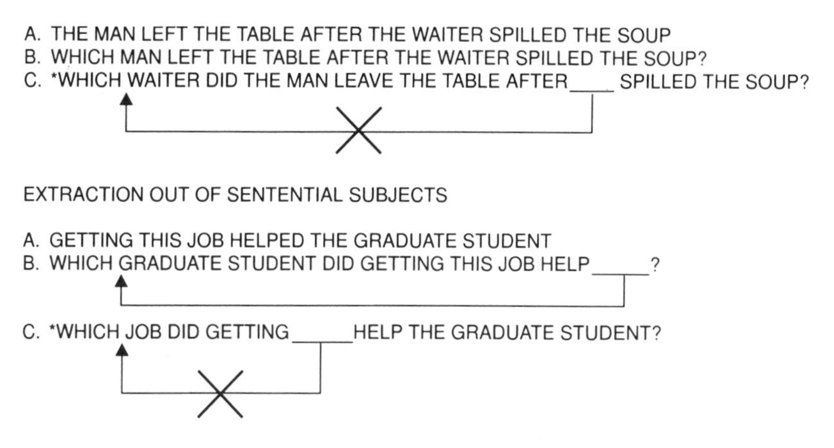

Figure 6.3 Extraction out of adjunct clauses and sententil subjects

instantiated in the L1 remain available to adult L2 learners, strongly suggesting that UG is not affected by a critical period.

Additional evidence for the role of the biologically endowed faculty for language comes from certain types of errors adult L2 learners make. To illustrate this we will return to the question of parameter-setting. Recall that in a parameter-setting model of language acquisition the child would set her parameter values for the L1 according to the data available in her linguistic environment. For the Branching Direction parameter, for example, the Japanese child would, upon hearing a few left-branching structures, set the value at Left Branching (LB). Under a Critical Period Hypothesis for principles and parameters, parameter-values that have not been set during L1 acquisition would no longer be available after a certain age. This would mean that adult Japanese speakers learning English would not have access to right-branching structures, only left-branching ones, since this is what is available in Japanese. Recall that English is principally a right-branching language. In addition, as shown in papers in Lust (1987) for L1 acquisition,

Table 6.1 Mean percent rejection of *wh*-extractions

	Relative Clause	*Adjunct Clause*	*Sentential Subjects*
Indonesian	90%	90%	84%
Chinese	73%	88%	83%

learners want to calibrate branching direction and anaphora direction. By anaphora direction we mean simply whether a pronoun precedes an antecedent or follows it. So in a right-branching language like English, a first language learner wants a pronoun to follow its antecedent as in the sentence in (5).

(5) When Ernie saw the clown, he laughed.

In left-branching languages a first language learner wants the pronoun to precede the antecedent, as shown in (6).

(6) When he saw the clown, Ernie laughed.

Utilising branching direction as a basis for predictions about second language acquisition, we would expect under a Critical Period Hypothesis that left-branching sentence structures in English should not be particularly problematic for a Japanese speaker to acquire, since what is available to the learner is the L1 which is left-branching. In addition, if this were true, we would predict that the patterns of acquisition that would emerge for the Japanese L2 learners should not resemble that for child first language learners of English who are able to access right-branching structures.

Contrary to these predictions, Flynn (1983, 1987) found that the sentence in (7) below is extremely difficult for adult Japanese speakers learning English.

(7) When the doctor received the results, he called the gentleman.

This sentence involves a pre-posed, left-branching adverbial adjunct clause as well as forward anaphora in which the antecedent *the doctor* precedes the pronoun *he*. These sentences do not involve a contrast in surface language facts between the L1 and the L2. They are productively licensed in Japanese — as exemplified in (8).

(8) Taroo wa nyuusi no kekka o kiita toki Ø hahaaoya ni denwa sita

Taroo-topic entrance exam-pos. result-acc. heard when Ø mother-dat. telephone did

'When Taroo heard (found out) the results of the entrance exam, (he) called his mother.'

In addition, these sentences are left-branching in accord with Japanese as principally a left-branching or head-final language. A second language acquisition model which derives language knowledge from the L1 only, therefore, does not predict the massive error rate made in imitation on these sentences as shown in Table 6.2.

Table 6.2 Mean amount correct imitation

Proficiency Level	*Low*	*Mid*	*High*
Score	0.00	0.16	0.95

(highest possible score = 3)

This error rate, we argue, is predicted by a parameter-setting model of L2 learning which is constrained by syntactic principles and parameters of UG. As already seen earlier, the Japanese speaker learning English must assign a new parameter setting for branching direction. If the Japanese L2 acquisition of English is constrained by the same parameters as is child L1 acquisition and if the L2 learner draws the same deductive consequences as the L1 learner, then errors on sentences as in (6) above can be explained since they not only offend parameter resetting for the L2 but they also offend the deductive consequence regarding anaphora direction which follows from the parameter setting. On the other hand, results such as these are left unaccounted for within a critical period formulation for syntactic principles and parameters of UG.

To summarise, we have argued that the evidence from experimental studies testing some syntactic principles of the language faculty supports a model of second language acquisition in which the biologically endowed language faculty is intact and operative, and we have given two examples of how aspects of this can be used to account for certain patterns of L2 acquisition. Thus, a model of second language acquisition which allows access to this faculty can in some sense explain the course of acquisition that critical period models cannot.

The question that now remains to be answered is: What explains the observed differences between native speakers and non-native speakers, both in the treatment of movement constraints and perhaps in proficiency in general? In other words, why do non-native speakers not perform at 100% levels as one might expect from native speakers?

It has been argued that this difference can only be accounted for by assuming a critical period for the language faculty. Such an explanation derives, we argue, from a basic misconception about the role of the language faculty in acquisition. The role of the language faculty, as we mentioned earlier, is to constrain acquisition so as to make it possible in the first place. At the same time, there are many other aspects in the acquisition process which we have called inductive processes and which do not derive from the language faculty. We note here again some phenomena such as lexical learning, and language-specific rules, i.e. things that are properly considered outside the domain of this faculty. Clearly, however, all aspects of language acquisition must interact in order to result in language proficiency. There is a whole process which leads the learner from having accessibility to a principle of the language faculty to mastering the particular instantiation of that principle in the language (e.g. identifying the sets of structures the principle ranges over — for instance, assimilating the fact that branching direction applies not only in relative clauses but in other complex sentences as well, for instance sentences with adverbial clauses).

The interaction between the various components of the language acquisition process was presented earlier in schematic form in Figure 6.1, where the dashed arrows represent the auxiliary processes needed to map the principles of the language faculty onto the particular demands of the language. Such processes, which are necessarily inductive in nature, could at least partially account for the observed differences between native and non-native speakers.

To briefly outline this proposal, we suggest the following: Because L2 learners already possess an L1 grammar, they hold confirmed beliefs about how each principle and parameter works as well as their domain of application for the construction of the L1 grammar. Application of the principles and parameters in turn involves extensive ancillary knowledge of the lexicon, etc. and idiosyncratic rules of the language (essentially tied to learned language-specific facts). The L2 learner, thus, is forced to shift not only hypotheses concerning principles and parameters but a whole range of interrelated language specific facts. The native speaker, in contrast, has already instantiated all principles and parameters in the context of a specific language. In other words, they have already gone through the process that we are now trying to explain for the adult L2 learner. In addition, the native speaker is not hindered by competing grammatical systems. In adult L2 learning, the instantiation of principles and parameters in the L2 may not be problematic but rather the mapping of the principles and the parameters onto the structures of the new target language. This mapping will take time as it of necessity involves inductive learning (see Lust, 1981).

The Language Faculty in the Domain of Phonology

Let us now turn to a consideration of some evidence from the acquisition of phonology, an area for which claims of a critical period have traditionally been the most persistent. Today it remains a widely held belief, both amongst laymen and L2 professionals, that beyond a certain age, often cited as puberty, and more recently as early as 5–7, it is impossible to acquire native-like pronunciation in a second or foreign language. Crucially, this inability is claimed to be biologically determined.

In the 1970s and 1980s a series of experimental studies investigated age-related differences in the acquisition of phonology, focusing in particular on L2 pronunciation. While some of these studies showed a positive correlation between age of arrival and degree of foreign accent as perceived by native speaker judges (e.g. Asher & García, 1982; Seliger, Krashen & Ladefoged, 1982; Oyama, 1982a, 1982b; Tahta *et al.*, 1981), others (e.g. Olson & Samuels, 1982; Snow & Hoefnagel-Höhle, 1982; Scovel, 1988) report that adults and adolescents in fact performed better than young children. An explanation that has been offered for these seemingly contradictory results is that these studies measure different phonological abilities (Krashen, Scarcella & Long, 1982). In particular, those studies which show an advantage for younger learners have been termed 'ultimate attainment studies', while those studies which showed an advantage for older acquirers age have been termed 'rate of acquisition' studies. It has been suggested that, because ultimate attainment studies measure long-term abilities, while rate of acquisition studies measure short-term abilities, the former are more reliable predictors of overall phonological abilities (Long, 1990).

In this section we argue that while the neurological evidence for a critical period for the acquisition of phonology remains speculative (e.g. Walsh & Diller, 1986; Seliger *et al.*, 1982 ; Obler & Macnamara, 1991), the empirical evidence available to us today points to the fact that general phonological abilities are maintained in adulthood and remain available to mature L2 learners. In particular, we will address our remarks to the biologically determined ability to construct new phonological systems. First, we will make more precise what this ability must consist of and, concomitantly, what the prediction of the loss of this ability entails for L2 acquisition. We will then suggest (*contra* Long, 1990) that ultimate attainment studies, measuring native-like pronunciation, may in fact not be the best way to measure this ability. Finally, we will consider some evidence from the area of L2 speech perception and production which indicate (i) that the biological ability underlying the construction of sound systems remains intact throughout one's lifespan, and (ii) that age-related differences are best explained within a multi-tiered speech learning model which assumes differential use of several processing modes.

Early speculation about a critical period for speech rested heavily on the assumption that speech abilities are related to hemispheric specialisation, and, crucially, that this specialisation is completed around puberty (Lenneberg, 1967). The original evidence for this assumption was the observation that when young children sustain left-hemisphere damage, they are able to recover speech using the right hemisphere, and that such recovery is less likely for adults. More evidence came from dichotic listening tasks, which seemed to indicate that adults exhibit more left-hemisphere dominance for speech than do children, thus again pointing to increased hemispheric specialisation in adulthood. However, in a recent review of brain damage and dichotic listening phenomena, Witelson (1987) concludes that, in fact, hemisphere specialisation exists in very young infants — at least as early as one month of age. She argues that there is no increase in lateralisation with age. Rather, she claims that there may be, in general, a gradual loss in the plasticity in the brain. With increasing age, if one area of the brain is damaged, other parts are less able to take over the functions previously dealt with by the damaged part.

Other hypotheses have suggested multiple critical periods, governing different subdomains of language. Such hypotheses were motivated by what seemed to be a discrepancy between the upper age limit in the acquisition of phonology (around 5 or 6) on the one hand, and that of syntax and the lexicon on the other (around 15 and upwards). Walsh & Diller (1986), for example, suggest that the two domains of language are subserved by different braincell types; phonology, a lower-order linguistic function, is on this view subserved by pyramidal cells, so-named because of their shape, while higher-order domains like morphology and syntax are subserved by stellate cells. Pyramidal cells adhere to a different maturational time schedule from that of stellate cells. Thus, the former cease to develop at the age of 6 or 7, while the latter continue to develop well into young adulthood. Seliger (1982) offers a similar hypothesis, based on differential schedules of localisation and lateralisation of the neurological substrates subserving the different linguistic subdomains. In a more recent review of the literature, Long (1990) suggests that because of its duration and progressive nature, myelination offers an attractive potential explanation for the gradual decline in the ability to achieve native-like pronunciation. In the same article he suggests that ultimate attainment studies, measuring long-term ability to achieve native-like pronunciation, constitute more relevant evidence for the acquisition of phonology than do rate of acquisition studies. He argues that pairing the behavioural evidence from ultimate attainment studies with the hypothetical neurophysiological events proposed by Walsh & Diller (1986) and Seliger *et al.* (1982) provides a strong argument for a Critical Period Hypothesis in the acquisition of phonology.

While the correlation proposed by Long may indeed prove useful in explaining the increased difficulty in achieving native-like pronunciation with age, we argue that native-like pronunciation is not an adequate measure of phonological competence. In general, linguistic competence determines potential abilities, rather than actualised proficiency. For the acquisition of phonology and in particular the cognition of speech sound, we would expect competence to govern more fundamental aspects such as, for example, the underlying ability to construct new sound systems. To sketch out this idea in some more detail, let us borrow some notions from another area of cognition, namely vision. Research in this cognitive domain has shown that the visual cortex is equipped with neurons which are specialised in the detection of features particular to the visual world, e.g. lines, contours, etc. Walsh & Diller (1986) have suggested that the same might be the case for language, and discuss the potential existence of neural detectors specialised for linguistic features. Following their suggestion, one would expect that in the case of phonology such neural detectors be specialised for the detection of phonetic and acoustic features pertinent to phonemic differentiation, since these constitute the crucial steps in the construction of a phonological system. That is, whatever else phonological competence may include[2], for speech cognition it would seem that the relevant underlying ability is not to be measured by eventual attainment of native-like pronunciation, but by a more fundamental ability, namely, the ability to detect sounds pertinent to speech and to manipulate or integrate them into a systematic mental representation of the sound system for the language being acquired. That this ability is indeed basic has been shown in early research in sound perception where newborn infants demonstrated an ability to distinguish speech sounds from non-speech sounds, as well as an ability to perceive distinctive features such as +/- voice (ba/pa) (Eimas *et al.*, 1974).

It is of course possible that the neurological substrate underlying this ability adheres to a maturational schedule, and that after maturation, presumably once the phonemic system of the L1 is well in place, its main function (i.e. the ability to detect distinctive features) diminishes or disappears. The next question to ask then, is: What sort of behavioural evidence would indicate that this basic ability changes with age? The required behavioural evidence, we argue, would be a decline over age in the sensory abilities to establish a new sound system, rather than the sensory abilities to fine-tune such a system. Thus, we would expect a loss or decline in phonological competence to result, for example, in the inability to detect and integrate the phonetic and acoustic features necessary to establish new phonemic contrasts. For L2 acquisition a fundamental change in these sensory abilities would result in a drastic reduction or even loss of a sensitivity to sound contrasts which do not exist in the L1. This would predict that only those contrasts which already exist in the L1 system should be available to the adult L2 learner.

In fact, research has shown that the sensory abilities to establish new contrasts remain intact in both perception and production. Interestingly, the evidence comes partly from the 'rate of acquisition' studies mentioned earlier, which showed that older learners (adolescents and adults) in fact have an advantage over younger learners in the short term. For example, Snow &Hoefnagel-Höhle (1982) tested, amongst other things, the production of Dutch /uy/ and /x/, phonemes that do not exist in English, by native speakers of English in both a laboratory and a naturalistic setting. In these studies, adults and older children (12–15) generally did better than younger children. Although results such as these are often ignored in favour of 'ultimate attainment' studies (where early L2 learners fare better than late ones), they in fact constitute an important piece of evidence which addresses directly the question of ability to produce or perceive novel sounds.

More recent research in psychoacoustic perception also argues against a decline in these fundamental sensory abilities. Thus, completely new phonemic categories in the L2, or so-called 'unequivalent sounds' (because they do not have an equivalent in the L1) are quite easily perceived by non-native speakers. For example, Best, McRoberts & Sithole (1988) report that a completely novel sound, such as the Kikuyu click is to native speakers of English, is perceived equally well by infants and adults whose L1 is English. Similarly, Werker & Tees (1983) show that novel contrasts, such as th/dh, which is phonemic in Hindu but not in English, is easily detected by both infants and adults whose L1 is English. While younger subjects fare somewhat better, Werker & Tees also show that with training adults can reach criterion in the perception of these contrasts. Data such as these would not be obtainable if the sensory abilities to perceive novel contrasts disappeared with age.

Similar arguments can be adduced for the production of novel sounds. If one were to lose the ability to perceive/produce new sound categories, we would expect those categories to be 'unlearnable'. However, adults can and do learn not only to perceive but also to produce new sounds. An early study by Neufeld (1977), for example, reports that some native speakers of English reached criterion in the production of Chinese, Japanese and French phrases, to the point of being perceived as native speakers by the listening judges. Similarly, Flynn & Manuel (1991) successfully trained Japanese subjects to both perceive and produce the English r/l distinction, which is non-phonemic in the L1. We reiterate that this demonstrated ability to achieve native-like proficiency, with training both in production and perception, is clearly incompatible with a loss in competence, either total or partial.

Further evidence that adults retain access to their original sensory abilities can be found in the work of Flege and his colleagues (Flege & Port, 1981; Port & Mitleb, 1980; Nathan, 1987; Flege, 1987) on voice onset time or VOT values. They found that L2 learners produce stops with a VOT value which lies between that of their L1 and the L2. For example, English /t/ has a long-lag VOT while Spanish /t/ has a short-lag VOT. When asked to pronounce English /t/, native speakers of Spanish learning English typically produce it with a VOT value which lies between English and Spanish, i.e. significantly lower than that of native speakers, but also significantly higher than that of the Spanish /t/. While a proficiency-oriented approach might focus on the fact that these learners did not produce native-like VOTs, the more significant points, as noted by Flege, are (1) that they were able to perceive the difference between the VOTs in the L1 and the L2 in the first place, and (2) that they were able to alter their production of these sounds from the way they are realised in the L1. Again, an explanation based on the loss of basic sensory abilities is inadequate here, as clearly these learners were able to identify and approximate phonetic features which differ in the L1 and the L2. Hypotheses have been advanced that there is an upper limit to the production of L2 VOTs. This is however contradicted by studies which show that some L2 learners do not differ from native speakers in their production of stops, or 'overshoot' native-speaker values (Suomi, 1980; Major, 1987; Flege & Eefting, 1986).

The evidence we have cited so far clearly does not support a loss or a change in the abilities to produce and perceive new sound contrasts; that is, in what we have argued to be fundamental aspects of phonological competence. However, as in the case of the acquisition of syntax, the question of course remains: What accounts for the observed difference between early and late learners? Here again, psychoacoustic research can help provide an answer. In a recent review of the literature, Wode (1991) suggests that the explanation lies in the interaction of different processing modes involved in establishing the phonemic system, namely the categorial/phonemic mode, the continuous/phonetic mode and the acoustic mode. In what follows, we will very briefly adumbrate this idea.

Setting up a phonemic system critically involves establishing discrete categories of sound which are meaningful in the ambient language (categorial/phonemic mode). To do this, the language learner uses the continuous/phonetic and acoustic modes. The process consists of using phonetic features to establish phonemic categories and then selectively and progressively shifting attention away from phonetic contrasts which are not meaningful in the language. This occurs from a very early age, as demonstrated in the research by Kuhl (1986). Thus, infants as young as 6 months of age pay more attention to contrasts that are non-phonemic in the ambient language than do older children, but gradually pay less attention to such cues for processing reasons. Crucially, however, the ultimate establishment of phonemic categories continues into adolescence and young adulthood (Flege & Eefting, 1987).

The difficulty in building a new phonological system for the L2 then, lies in *reversing* the process used to establish the L1 system. Thus, in constructing a new system, the learner has to relearn to focus on phonetic contrasts. For example, sounds which already constitute a phonemic category in the L1, such as /p/t/k/ in English, typically show an age effect. Werker & Tees (1983), for example, show that English speaking adults are much worse than infants in detecting a difference between dental and retroflex t, a contrast which is phonemic in Hindi but not English or velar vs. glottalised k, a contrast which is phonemic in a native American language Thompson. However, the age difference seems to vary with the particular contrasts in question. Notice that this is a very different argument from that made by the Critical Period Hypothesis, which says that the basic abilities to establish a phonemic system are lost or fundamentally altered. Crucially, the studies we mentioned above show that all three modes (phonemic, phonetic and acoustic) are accessible to adults in identifying non-native sounds (Werker & Logan, 1985).

Conclusion

To conclude, in this chapter we have argued on the basis of the acquisition of aspects of syntax and phonology, that the biologically determined faculty for language — i.e. competence — remains accessible to adult learners, and that differences between child and adult learners can be derived from the ancillary processes used to instantiate competence into the particular demands of a language (e.g. the L2). Understanding and articulating the issues in this way allows us to reconcile different aspects of what we observe about adults in language acquisition, specifically, the fact that in spite of showing solid knowledge of principles and parameters in the area of syntax and retaining critical sensory abilities for constructing phonemic systems, adult second language learners may at times fail to reach native proficiency in either or both areas. A sweeping biological explanation, we submit, fails to answer the more subtle and ultimately more interesting question of what particular aspects of linguistic behaviour are affected by age.

Notes

1. For a more in-depth discussion of these issues the reader is referred to Hornstein & Lightfoot (1981).
2. We refer here to the even 'deeper' properties of the phonological competence, such as principles and parameters governing the mental representation of rule systems.

References

ASHER, J. and GARCÍA, R. 1982, The optimal age to learn a foreign language. In S. KRASHEN, R. SCARCELLA and M. LONG (eds) *Child–Adult Differences in Second Language Acquisition* (pp. 3–12). Rowley, MA: Newbury House.

BEST, C., McROBERTS, G. and SITHOLE, N. 1988, Examination of perceptual reorganization for nonnative speech contrasts: Zulu click discrimination by English-speaking adults and infants. *Journal of Experimental Psychology* 14, 345–60.

CHOMSKY, N. 1968, *Language and Mind*. New York: Harcourt, Brace Jovanovitch.

— 1973, Conditions on transformations. In S. ANDERSON and P. KIPARSKY (eds) *A Festschrift for Morris Halle*. New York: Holt, Rinehart and Winston.

EIMAS, P.D., SIQUELAND, E.R., JUSCZYK, P. and VIGORITO, J. 1971, Speech perception in infants. *Science* 171, 303–6.

FLEGE, J.E. 1987, The production of 'new' and 'similar' phones in a foreign language: Evidence for the effect of effect of equivalence classification. *Journal of Phonetics* 15, 47–65.

— 1991, Age of learning affects the authenticity of voice-onset time (VOT) in stop consonants produced in a second language. *Journal of the Acoustical Society of America* 89, 295–411.

FLEGE, J.E. and EEFTING, W.Z. 1986, Linguistic and developmental effects on the production and perception of stop consonants. *Phonetica* 43, 155–71.

FLEGE, J.E. and PORT, R. 1981, Cross-language phonetic interference: Arabic to English. *Language Speech* 28, 81–92.

FLYNN, S. 1983, Study of the effects of principal branching direction in second language acquisition: The generalization of a parameter of universal grammar from first to second language acquisition. Unpublished PhD dissertation, Cornell University.

— 1987, *A Parameter-Setting Model of L2 Acquisition*. Dordrecht: Reidel.

FLYNN, S. and MANUEL, S. 1991, Age-dependent effects in language acquisition: An evaluation of 'Critical Period' Hypotheses. In L. EUBANK (ed.) *Point/Counterpoint: Universal Grammar in the Second Language* (pp. 117–46). Amsterdam: John Benjamins.

KRASHEN., S., SCARCELLA., R. and LONG, M. (eds) 1982, *Child–Adult Differences in Second Language Acquisition*. Rowley, MA: Newbury House.

KUHL, P.K. 1986, Reflections on infants' perception and representation of speech. In J.S. PERKELL and D.H. KLATT (eds) *Invariance and Variability in Speech Processes* (pp. 19–30). Hillsdale, NJ: Lawrence Erlbaum.

LENNEBERG, E. 1967, *Biological Foundations of Language*. New York: Wiley.

LONG, M.H. 1990, Maturational constraints on language development. *Studies in Second Language Acquisition* 12, 251–85.

LOWIE, W. 1988, Age and foreign language pronunciation in the classroom. Unpublished thesis, University of Amsterdam.

LUST, B. (ed.) 1987, *Studies in the Acquisition of Anaphora*. Dordrecht: Reidel.

MAJOR, R. 1987, English voiceless stop production by speakers of Brazilian Portuguese. *Journal of Phonetics* 15, 197–202.

MARTOHARDJONO, G. 1993, Wh-movement in the acquisition of a second language: A cross-linguistic study of three languages with and without syntactic movement. Unpublished PhD dissertation, Cornell University

MARTOHARDJONO, G. and GAIR, J.W. 1993, Apparent UG inaccessibility in second language acquisition: Misapplied principles or principled misapplications? In F. ECKMAN (ed.) *Confluence: Linguistics, L2 Acquisition and Speech Pathology* (pp. 79–103). Amsterdam: John Benjamins.

NATHAN, G. 1987, On second language acquisition and voiced stops. *Journal of Phonetics* 15, 313–22.

NEUFELD, G. 1977, Language learning ability in adults: A study on the acquisition of prosodic and articulatory features. *Working Papers on Bilingualism* 12, 46–60.

OBLER, L. and MACNAMARA, P. 1991, Neurological evidence concerning a critical period for second language acquisition. Paper presented at the Annual Meeting of the American Association for the Advancement of Science, Washington, DC, January 1991.

OLSON, L. and SAMUELS, S.J. 1982, The relationship between age and accuracy of foreign language pronunciation. In S. KRASHEN., R. SCARCELLA. and M. LONG (eds) *Child–Adult Differences in Second Language Acquisition* (pp. 67–75). Rowley, MA: Newbury House.

OYAMA, S. 1982a, A sensitive period for the acquisition of a nonative phonological system. In S. KRASHEN, R. SCARCELLA. and M. LONG (eds) *Child–Adult Differences in Second Language Acquisition* (pp. 20–38). Rowley, MA: Newbury House.

— 1982b, The sensitive period and comprehension of speech. In S. KRASHEN, R. SCARCELLA. and M. LONG (eds) *Child–Adult Differences in Second Language Acquisition* (pp. 39–51). Rowley, MA: Newbury House.

PORT, R. and MITLEB, F. 1980, Phonetic and phonological manifestation of the voicing contrast in Arabic-accented English. *Research in Phonetics 1, 137–65.*

SCOVEL, T. 1988, *A Time to Speak: A Psycholinguistic Inquiry into the Critical Period for Human Speech*. New York: Harper and Row.

SELIGER, H. W. 1982, On the possible role of the right hemisphere in second language acquisition. *TESOL Quarterly* 16, 307–14.

SELIGER, H.W., KRASHEN, S.D. and LADEFOGED, P. 1982, Maturational constraints on the acquisition of second language accent. In S. KRASHEN, R. SCARCELLA and M. LONG (eds) *Child–Adult Differences in Second Language Acquisition* (pp.13–20). Rowley, MA: Newbury House.

SNOW, C. and HOEFNAGEL-HÖHLE, M. 1982, The critical period for language acquisition: evidence from second language learning. In S. KRASHEN, R. SCARCELLA and M. LONG (eds) *Child–Adult Differences in Second Language Acquisition* (pp. 93–111). Rowley, MA: Newbury House.

SUOMI, K. 1980, *Voicing in English and Finnish Stops*. Publication 10 of the Department of English and General Linguistics, Turku University, Finland.

TAHTA, S., WOOD, M. and LOEWENTHAL, K. 1981, Foreign accents: Factors relating to transfer of accent from the first language to a second language. *Language and Speech* 24, 265–72.

WALSH, T. and DILLER, K. 1986, Neurolinguistic considerations on the optimum age for second language learning. In K. DILLER (ed.) *Individual Differences and Universals in Language Learning Aptitude* (pp. 3–21). Rowley, MA: Newbury House.

WERKER, J.F. and LOGAN, J.S. 1985, Cross-language evidence for three factors in speech perception. *Perception and Psychophysics* 37, 35–44.

WERKER, J.F. and TEES, R. 1983, Developmental changes across childhood in the perception of non-native sounds. *Canadian Journal of Psychology* 37 (2), 278–86.

WITELSON, S. 1987, Early hemisphere specialization and interhemispheric plasticity: An empirical and theoretical review. In S.J. SEGALOWITZ and F.A. GRUBER (eds) *Language Development and Neurological Theory* (pp. 213–37). New York: Academic Press.

WODE, H. 1991. Speech perception: A developmental perspective. Unpublished manuscript, English Departmet and Center for Bilingualism and Language Contact, Kiel University.

Index

3430